D112583S

Caribbean Pirates

Warren Alleyne

CARIBBEAN

Macmillan Education
Between Towns Road, Oxford OX4 3PP
A division of Macmillan Publishers Limited
Companies and representatives throughout the world

ISBN- 13: 978-0-333-40584-0

ISBN- 10: 0-333-40584-6

Copyright text © W.Alleyne 1986
Design and illustration © Macmillan Publishers Limited 1986

First published 1986

All rights reserved; no part of this publication may be
reproduced, stored in a retrieval system, transmitted in any
form or by any means, electronic, mechanical, photocopying,
recording, or otherwise, without the prior written permission
of the Publishers.

www.macmillan-caribbean.com

Printed and bound in Thailand

2010 2009 2008 2007 2006
24 23 22 21 20 19 18

Contents

Acknowledgements

The author and publishers wish to acknowledge, with thanks, the following photographic sources:

The Barbados Museum and Historical Society   p 5

BBC Hulton Picture Library   pp 38; 103

British Library, British Museum, London   p 34

Library of Congress U.S.A.   pp 50, 61, 99

Mansell Collection   pp 11, 19, 23, 80, 96

Mary Evans Picture Library   p 28

Peabody Museum of Salem, U.S.A.   p 69

Public Record Office, Nassau   p 47

Cover illustration - George Craig

The publishers have made every effort to trace the copyright holders, but if they have inadvertently overlooked any, they will be pleased to make the necessary arrangements at the first opportunity.

Preface

The main contemporary sources of material on pirates and piracy are Daniel Defoe's *A General History of the Pirates* and Alexander O. Exquemelin's *The Buccaneers of America*. Originally published in 1724, the *General History*, edited by Manuel Schonhorn, was republished in 1972 by Messrs J.M. Dent and Sons Ltd of London. Exquemelin's classic was originally published in 1678, in Dutch, and the first translation into English, from a Spanish version of 1681, appeared in 1684. Other English editions have followed from time to time, and one of the most recent, translated from the Dutch by Alexis Brown, was published by Penguin Books in 1969.

Much useful contemporary material of the period 1714-1730, generally regarded as the golden age of piracy, is also to be found in the official documents reproduced in the Calendar of State Papers, Colonial; America and the West Indies, Volumes XXVII -XXXVII. Also quite useful is *The Pirates of the New England Coast, 1630-1730*, by George Francis Dow and John Henry Edmonds. Although not itself a contemporary work, having first appeared in 1923, it is based upon court records and other original documents, including newspapers, in the Massachusetts State Archives. This work was republished in 1968 by Argosy-Antiquarian Ltd of New York.

A great deal has been written on the subject of piracy, and interested readers are recommended to consult the lengthy bibliographies contained in such books as *The Pirates*, by Douglas Botting and the Editors of Time-Life Books, published by Time-Life Books, Alexandria, Virginia, 1978; and *Blackbeard the Pirate*, by Robert E. Lee, published by John F. Blair, Winston-Salem, North Carolina (second edition, 1976).

W.A.

Introduction

Piracy has existed ever since man built boats and ventured upon the seas. There were pirates in the time of Homer, and the Roman lawyer Cicero (106-43 BC) dubbed them 'enemies of the human race'.

Piracy is robbery at sea. The counterparts of pirates on land go by many names - bandits, brigands, highwaymen, to mention but a few of them. The common characteristic of all such persons is that they are acting on their own behalf for personal gain; they rob indiscriminately; they are outlaws of society and they have allegiance to nobody except their associates in crime.

From quite an early date we find sea marauders who deviate from this narrow definition. The Vikings of Scandinavia, for example, who sailed to the coasts of the British Isles and France from the 8th to the 10th century AD, plundering ships and towns, began as pirates but eventually became agents of national expansion, acting with the approval and support of the country from which they came. Much the same is true of the well-known Barbary pirates or 'corsairs', who came into prominence in the 16th century and were the scourge of the Mediterranean and further afield until they were finally stamped out in 1830, when France captured Algiers, their chief stronghold.

The origin of the Barbary pirates can be traced to the Muhammedan conquest of the north coast of Africa. When the Moors were expelled from Spain in 1492 they began piratical attacks on the Spanish coast. These developed into attacks on Christians as a whole; the Moors seized their

1

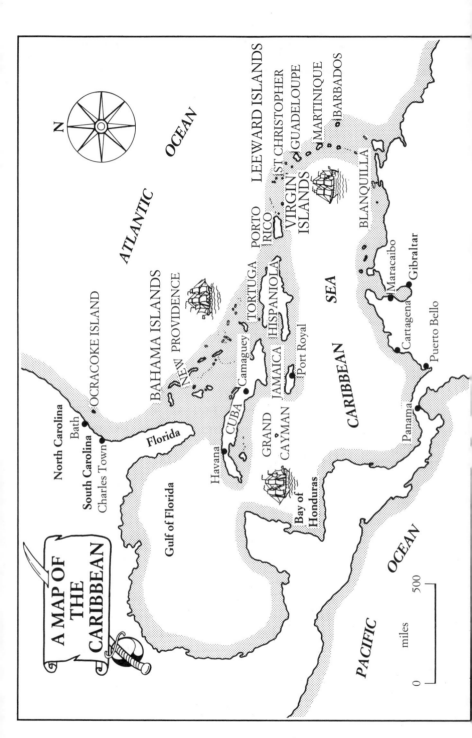

A MAP OF THE CARIBBEAN

N

ATLANTIC OCEAN

North Carolina
Bath
South Carolina
Charles Town

Florida

Gulf of Florida

Havana

CUBA

BAHAMA ISLANDS

NEW PROVIDENCE

OCRACOKE ISLAND

Camaguey

TORTUGA

HISPANIOLA

PORTO RICO

LEEWARD ISLANDS

ST CHRISTOPHER
GUADELOUPE
VIRGIN ISLANDS

MARTINIQUE

BARBADOS

JAMAICA

Port Royal

GRAND CAYMAN

Bay of Honduras

CARIBBEAN SEA

BLANQUILLA

Maracaibo
Gibraltar

Cartagena

Puerto Bello

Panama

PACIFIC OCEAN

0   500
miles

2

property and sold the Christians themselves as slaves.

As a result of the discovery of the West Indies by Columbus in 1492 a new situation was created. On the strength of a Papal Bull which was subsequently confirmed by a treaty between Spain and Portugal, Spain claimed ownership of all lands in the Caribbean and for more than a century and a half she tried to deny the right of ships of any other country to enter the area, even for purposes of trade. The Spanish claim was never admitted by other European nations, and first the French, later the English and the Dutch, sent their ships to plunder Spanish settlements and capture Spanish vessels. Most of these ships operated with the full sanction of their governments, which issued to them 'Letters of Marque' specifically authorising hostile action against Spain.

Such ships, which were not pirate ships but really naval auxiliaries, were known as 'privateers'. Actually, there had been privateers for several centuries. In the days when national navies were small, privately-owned merchant ships were pressed into service in time of war and formed part of the national fleet. The innovation in the 16th century was the authorisation of merchant ships to operate independently or in small groups against one country, Spain, in a part of the world far removed from any theatre of war.

The expression 'No peace beyond the line' is often used with reference to the Caribbean. What it meant was that hostilities between Spain and other European powers which took place outside European waters would not be regarded as justification for a general state of war with those nations. Sometimes it did lead to war; sometimes Spain went no further than to lay complaints. Eventually, however, Spain at least tacitly recognised the rights of other nations to lands which they found unoccupied and which they had occupied. One cannot give a precise date to this, but it was during the time that the buccaneers were active that one finds a change in attitude on the part of the British to raids on Spanish settlements and shipping.

The buccaneers, or 'boucaniers' – a French term meaning 'smokers of meat' – were operating by the early 1660's, preying on Spanish commerce. Though they included men of many nations they at first used Port Royal in Jamaica as their base. In 1664, when the Government of Jamaica prohibited their activities, they moved their headquarters to Tortuga, a small island off the north-west coast of Haiti (as it is now known). British policy towards the buccaneers vacillated; at one time it approved their activities and regarded them as privateers, at other times it condemned them as pirates. This explains how it came about that Henry Morgan, the most famous of the buccaneers, later received the accolade of knighthood and served with distinction as Lieutenant-Governor of Jamaica.

Piracy, in the true sense, began in the Caribbean when England and France began to establish settlements in the Lesser Antilles in the second quarter of the 17th century. In 1650, for example, an Irish pirate was operating off Barbados and even entered a harbour and stole a ship, as a result of which the authorities had to strengthen the island's coastal defences. As the name of the pirate captain was known in the island, he had probably been active in the area for some time.

As the century progressed, piracy must have become a serious menace, for in 1684 we find a law being passed in Barbados entitled 'How Pyrates and Felonies done upon the sea shall be tried and Punished'. The preamble to the law began:

> 'Forasmuch as several Colonies and Plantations belonging to our Most Gracious Sovereign, King Charles the Second in America, have been lately infested by a dangerous sort of People called Pirates, who are not only Enemies to them of His Majesty's Settlement, but of all Mankind...'

Like all robbers, pirates were the victims of greed. The lure of untold riches, easily won, was irresistible, and the dire penalties which would inevitably follow capture proved no deterrent. No doubt some who had served as privateers

Preamble.

FOrasmuch as several Colonies and Plantations belonging to our most Gracious Sovereign King *Charles* the Second in *America*, have been lately infested by a dangerous sort of People called Pirates, who are not only Enemies to them of His Majesty's Settlement, but of all Mankind: And for that the Persons said to be Pirates, are most commonly Thieves, Robbers, Murtherers and Man-slayers, and other Misdoers contrary to the known Laws. And to the intent that all such that shall be taken in or about this Island, or brought Prisoners hither, may be proceeded against according to the Statute made in the Twenty Eighth Year of *Henry* the Eighth, Declaring and Enacting how Pirates on the Seas shall be Tried and Punished.

Clause I.

Be it therefore Enacted by his Excellency, Sir *Richard Dutton*, Knight, Captain General, and Governour in Chief of this and other the *Charibbee-Islands*, the Honourable the Council and General Assembly of this Island, and by Authority of the same, That whatsoever Person or Persons that are or shall be taken, sent or brought to this Island Prisoners, for having committed Treason, Felonies, Pyracies or other Offences upon the Seas, or in any Creek, Haven or Bay in or about this Island, shall be inquired, heard, tryed and determined in this Island, in such Form and Manner, as if such Offences had been committed, perpetrated and

Treason, Pyracy, &c. to be tried as Offences at Land. done upon the Land, by virtue of a Commission under His Majesty's Seal appointed for this and other the *Charibbee-Islands*, signed by His Majesty's Governour or Commander in Chief here for the time being, impowering one Person to be chief Judge, together with Five or more substantial Persons by him in the said Commission to be appointed, to hear, try and determine the Offences aforesaid, after the common course of the Laws of the Kingdom of *England*. And such as shall be convicted of any such Offence or Offences, by Verdict, Confession or Process, by Authority of any such Commission, shall have and suffer such Pains of Death, Loss of Lands Goods and Chattels, as if they had been attainted and convicted of any such Crimes and Offences done upon the Land : Any Law or Statute to the contrary notwithstanding.

Read, and pass'd the Council, and consented to by his Excellency, this 10th Day of *December*, 1684.

Read and pass'd the Assembly, this 10th Day of *December*, 1684, *Nemine contradicente.*

Edwin Stede, Deputy Secretary.   *Richard Cartwright*, Cl. of the Assemb.

An

Act Number 306 (The Laws of Barbados *William Rawlin*, 1699)

lapsed into piracy, and this is particularly true of the period beginning in 1713. During the War of the Spanish Succession - in America commonly called Queen Anne's War - piracy had declined, but when the Treaty of Utrecht brought the War to an end hundreds of seamen found themselves without employment, and many who had known no other calling than the legal plundering of enemy shipping now turned their hands to illegal plundering of all shipping. This goes a long way to explain why the years which followed saw the heyday of piracy in the Caribbean, producing such notorious pirate leaders as Benjamin Hornigold, Edward Teach (alias Blackbeard), John Rackham (alias Calico Jack), the women pirates Anne Bonney and Mary Read, and most powerful of all, perhaps, Bartholomew Roberts, to name just a few.

Because of the directions of the winds and currents, shipping leaving the Caribbean for Europe or North America had to make its way north through the Florida Channel off the east coast of Florida. To the east of the Channel lay the numerous small islands and cays which now form the Bahamas. At the beginning of the 18th century the islands were mostly unpopulated and they had been almost entirely neglected by the European powers, to whom they offered no attraction. They were, however, an ideal base for pirates. There were plenty of places where ships could be hidden and repaired and cleaned without danger of attack by naval vessels. Except perhaps in Madagascar in the Indian Ocean, or Algiers in the Mediterranean, there was probably a larger concentration of pirates in the Bahamas than anywhere in the world.

By the year 1717, the depredations of pirates had produced a paralysing effect on trade throughout the Caribbean. Writing in July that year to the Council of Trade and Plantations in London, the Governor of Barbados, Robert Lowther, stated:

> 'I cannot but doubt that your Lordships have heard that these parts are more infested with pirates than have been formerly known, and that they have already done much injury to trade in general as well as great damage to particular persons.'

The following month of August the Governor of Jamaica, Sir Nicholas Lawes, similarly reported to the Council that merchant ships of that island dared not venture to sea except in convoy under naval escort. Nine months later he was further to report that some thirty ships trading to Jamaica had recently been taken and plundered by pirates.

But pirates were not content merely to plunder ships of their cargoes and valuables. They often inflicted devilish tortures upon their prisoners. The cat-o-nine-tails, fire, and the rope were much favoured by them as instruments of torture; but generally they subjected their victims to whatever barbarities their brutal minds could devise. For example, Captain Edward North of the sloop *William and Martha*, which was captured and plundered by Charles Vane in April 1718, reported to the authorities at Bermuda that the pirates bound a member of the crew hand and foot and tied him upon his back down to the bowsprit, pushed a loaded pistol into his mouth, and held burning matches to his eyes to force him to disclose what money and valuables the vessel had on board.

The remedies proposed for this state of affairs were an increased naval force to police the seas and an amnesty, or pardon, to all pirates who should give themselves up within a given time. In September 1717, King George I, upon the advice of his Privy Council, decided to put both these measures into force. Additional ships of war were ordered to the West Indian and North American Colonies, whilst a proclamation was issued offering pardon to all pirates who should surrender not later than September 5th, 1718. Copies of this were despatched to all the colonial governors, who, of course, were authorised to accept surrenders and issue the certificates of pardon.

It happened that earlier that same year, 1717, Captain Woodes Rogers, a distinguished mariner who had sailed around the world between 1708 and 1711 in command of two privateers, had petitioned the King for a commission as Governor of the Bahamas, which then had no form of government and no settled inhabitants. His petition had the support of a large number of merchants trading with the

7

British colonies in America. Rogers requested a garrison of troops, some guns and military stores, as well as other provisions necessary for establishing a settlement. He duly obtained his commission, and finally arrived at New Providence in July 1718 accompanied by three naval vessels and a military contingent. Vested with full authority to suppress piracy in the area, he brought along the King's proclamation of pardon to all pirates who should surrender by the date specified.

Governor Rogers found several hundred pirates in the islands. These all surrendered and were given certificates of pardon - with the exception of Charles Vane and his crew, who sailed away defiantly flying their pirate flags. Benjamin Hornigold, who had accepted a pardon, took command of a sloop and went off in search of Vane, but never caught up with him.

The results of the King's pardon, however, proved disappointing for the majority of those who had accepted it, and a good many soon relapsed into their old way of life. This was partly because few persons were willing to employ them and partly because piracy offered an easier way to wealth than honest toil.

Piracy and other felonies committed at sea were matters that properly fell within the jurisdiction of the High Court of the British Admiralty; but during the 17th century difficulties often arose over the procedure for dealing with such offences when committed at considerable distances from Britiain. Offenders could be sent home for trial, but this involved delays, loss of witnesses, and risks of escape, so it is not surprising that attempts were made to try offenders in the Colonies, even though the legality of this was doubtful.

The matter was finally settled by a statute passed in 1700, in the reign of King William III, which without diminishing the jurisdiction of the High Court of Admiralty made it possible under the Great Seal or the Seal of the Admiralty to try piracy in America. Under this statute, which was renewed in the reign of Queen Anne and made perpetual in the reign of George I, courts for the trial of piracy were constituted and judges appointed by the Sovereign's Commission.

In most parts of the world piracy at sea no longer exists. However, a resurgence in the waters of South East Asia occurred in the late 1970s, when pirates operating in speedboats and trawlers, and armed with automatic weapons, began preying on fishing boats and small trading vessels. Occasionally they attacked larger ships as well, and since 1980 these attacks have increased so alarmingly that merchant ships belonging to certain countries are said now to carry marksmen on board for protection when trading to that area.

It is understood that a great many shipping companies and seamen's unions are opposed to the arming of merchant vessels, as was done in earlier times; consequently, some kind of anti-pirate force organised and controlled by the United Nations would appear to be necessary for patrolling the waters of any region where the threat of piracy exists.

Francis L'Olonnois

The sea rovers who, of old, infested the Caribbean Sea and the Spanish Main were generally a breed of fierce, hardbitten men, not noted for having any quality of mercy. But one who was unmatched by any other for savagery was the buccaneer called Francis L'Olonnois.

The real name of this demonic individual was Jean David Nau, and he was born in France, probably in the third decade of the 17th century. In his youth he was shipped to one of the West Indian islands as a bond-servant, having contracted to work for some planter or merchant for a certain number of years, and when his term expired he sailed to the island of Hispaniola, where he lived for a while among the hunters.

These men, who made a livelihood hunting the herds of cattle and pigs that ran wild in the forest, smoke-dried meat by a method learned from the native Carib Indians. The meat was hung in strips over a frame of green sticks and dried above a fire fed with animal bones and hide trimmings. This grid, as also the place where the curing was done, was called by the Carib name of 'boucan', and on this account the hunters became known as 'boucaniers', or 'buccaneers'.

In due course these buccaneers took to raiding Spanish coastal shipping, operating from dug-out canoes, but later, in captured vessels, they were able to venture further afield attacking Spanish ships on the high seas and raiding coastal settlements.

Francis L'Olonnois sailed on two or three voyages as one of these freebooters, and so distinguished himself by his

Francis L'Olonnois

courage that in 1667, when war broke out between France and Spain, the French Governor of Tortuga, an island off the northern coast of Hispaniola where the buccaneers had established themselves, gave him command of a ship and commissioned him to pillage the shipping of Spain.

In a short time not only had he made himself a fortune; he had also become notorious throughout the region on account of his savage cruelties against the Spaniards.

Eventually his ship was wrecked in a great storm on

the coast of Campeche, Mexico. He and his crew got safely to land, but the Spaniards attacked and killed most of them and took the rest prisoner. L'Olonnois, who was wounded, managed to avoid capture by concealing himself beneath the dead, and after hiding in the forest for a while he made his way into Campeche disguised as a Spaniard. He finally managed to return to Tortuga with the help of some slaves, who stole a canoe one night and carried him back after he had promised them their freedom as a reward.

By no means undaunted by his recent misfortunes, he was soon back at sea with 20 well-armed companions in a small vessel he had obtained by trickery. One day when he appeared off a small town on Cuba's northern coast with the intention of plundering the coastal vessels, some fishermen recognised him and hurried overland to Havana and reported his presence to the Governor. Having recently had letters from Campeche informing him that the brutal pirate, L'Olonnois, was dead, the Governor believed the men to be mistaken, but at their insistence he sent out a strong party of armed men in a small ship of ten guns with orders to capture and hang all the buccaneers except their leader, whom he wanted brought back alive.

But this vessel was herself attacked and boarded by L'Olonnois and his gang, who drove the Spaniards below deck. Then, calling them up one by one, L'Olonnois personally struck off each man's head as he emerged from the hatch, sparing only one prisoner, whom he sent back to the Governor with a message declaring that he would never give quarter to any Spaniard.

Now that he was in possession of a better ship, he recruited more men at Tortuga and sailed for Maracaibo, Venezuela, where, in the bay, he captured a ship on her way in to purchase a cargo of cocoa. She was found to have plenty of money and merchandise on board, and L'Olonnois returned in triumph to Tortuga and set about gathering a larger expedition to return and sack the city of Maracaibo itself, as well as all the neighbouring coastal towns and villages.

While en route off eastern Hispaniola in July 1668, this force numbering about 700 men in eight vessels sighted a ship outbound from Puerto Rico to Mexico, and L'Olonnois took off in pursuit and finally captured her after a stiff fight that lasted three hours.

She was found to be carrying 120,000 pounds weight in cocoa and 40,000 pieces of eight, as well as jewellery of a value of at least 10,000 pieces of eight. L'Olonnois sent her to Tortuga, where she was speedily unloaded and sent back with a cargo of provisions to the island of Savona (now Saona), where the expedition had paused to await her return.

The city of Maracaibo had been plundered by rovers about ten or twelve years previously; consequently, when this group of buccaneers arrived and entered, they found that the population had fled and gone into hiding. They were, however, able to feast and make merry on the large quantity of food, wine, and livestock that had been abandoned. Then, anxious to discover where the citizens had hidden their money and valuables, a large party went out next day to try to take prisoners and bring them in for questioning, and in the evening they returned with 20 persons, children as well as adults, 20,000 pieces of eight, and several mules laden with goods of various kinds.

On the following day several of the prisoners were tortured to force them to disclose where more money and goods were hidden. All, however, refused to talk; but when L'Olonnois angrily drew his cutlass and hacked one of them to pieces and threatened the others with the same fate if they persisted in remaining silent, one terrified man offered to lead the buccaneers to the place where the citizens were hiding. But the fugitives had taken the precaution of burying their goods and moving daily from one place to another, and the raiders failed to track them down.

After remaining 14 days at Maracaibo, the buccaneers

moved on to Gibraltar, a large village some 90 miles farther south, which they captured after several hours of fierce fighting. They left a month later, after forcing the population to pay a heavy ransom of 10,000 pieces of eight as the price of not burning the place to the ground, and then returned to Maracaibo, where they looted the warehouses and even the churches. Also, by similarly threatening to burn the city they succeeded in extorting 20,000 pieces of eight and 500 head of cattle from the defenceless citizens.

The spoil taken on this expedition, amounting to some 260,000 pieces of eight in cash, jewellery, and silver plate, was divided among the freebooters on an island off the south-western coast of Hispaniola, with each man receiving an additional bounty of at least 100 pieces of eight's worth of linen and silk goods and other small items. But less than a week after they got back to Tortuga, a good many of them had gambled away their shares of this ill-gotten harvest of wealth.

On account of the great prestige this enterprise had gained him, L'Olonnois had no difficulty in recruiting men for a new expedition he proposed to take to Nicaragua, and when he finally sailed he had a force of some 700 men on board his six vessels.

As these ships were unable to navigate the shallow River Nicaragua (now the San Juan River) the pirates called at a port on the south coast of Cuba, where they robbed the poor fishermen of a large number of canoes, and then set course for Cabo Gracias a Dios, the northernmost port on the coast of Nicaragua. But they failed to arrive, for the vessels ran into a calm and were carried by the currents north-westwards into the Gulf of Honduras.

Soon the company ran short of food and were driven by hunger into plundering all the towns and villages around the Gulf. Arriving, in due course, at the coastal town of Puerto Cavallo, they found and captured a heavily armed Spanish merchant ship, and then swarmed ashore and launched into an orgy of pillaging and burning. The prisoners taken were subjected to the most devilish cruelties. When a victim being tortured on the rack happened to be too slow in answering his questions, L'Olonnois would personally hack him to pieces with his cutlass and lick the blood from the blade like some crazy vampire.

Eventually, after most of the prisoners had perished at the hands of this inhuman creature, he found two who offered to guide him and a strong force of his men to San Pedro, an inland town.

About nine miles en route the buccaneers were ambushed by a party of Spaniards, but soon drove them off; and on learning from some of the prisoners taken that further ambushes had been set up L'Olonnois enquired whether there was any alternative route to the town. When the men replied that they knew of none he furiously ripped one of them open with his cutlass, tore his heart from his body, chewed on it, and then hurled it into the face of one of the others with a threat to treat him the same way unless he showed him another route. The terrified prisoners then agreed to guide him to another track, but pointed out that it was very difficult.

And, indeed, it proved so inaccessible that he and his men were forced to return to the original route and fight their way out of two more ambushes before they finally reached the town and launched an attack.

Before surrendering, after putting up a fierce resistance, the Spaniards called for a truce of two hours, and when the buccaneers finally entered the town they found that everything of value had been removed. Finally, they set the place on fire and committed all the usual atrocities before returning to the coast.

Shortly afterwards, his two principal lieutenants, who had become disappointed that the expedition had so far failed to reap the rich harvest of plunder they had been led to expect, decided to seek their fortunes independently elsewhere, and they sailed away leaving Francis L'Olonnois alone with his own ship and her crew of 300 men.

Not long afterwards this vessel ran aground on a reef on an islet, and unable to get her off, L'Olonnois was forced to break her up in order to obtain timber for building a longboat. As his companions realised that it would be some time before they would be able to get away they set about cultivating the ground and planting food crops.

When the longboat was completed it could not accommodate all the shipwrecked men, so it was decided to send a party to the mainland to try to capture and bring back a number of canoes sufficient to take off those men who were still on the island. L'Olonnois and his party, after a few days, finally arrived at the mouth of the River Nicaragua, but here they were set upon by both the Indians and the Spaniards, who killed several of them.

L'Olonnois and the other survivors then decided to take the boat along the coast of Cartagena in the hope of capturing a suitable vessel of some kind. But on their arrival in the Gulf of Darien they were all captured by a band of ferocious Indians, and the equally ferocious L'Olonnois, who had so often taken delight in hacking innocent persons to death and indulging in all kinds of gruesome atrocities, was himself hacked in pieces and roasted limb by limb.

The men who had been left on the islet off Nicaragua, having had no news of him since his departure, were delighted when a buccaneer expedition happened to call in on its way from Jamaica to the mainland and rescued them from the miserable existence they had been leading for the past ten months. And their rescuers, on their part, were equally pleased at so unexpectedly gaining additional strength for the raid they had planned on a city in the interior of Nicaragua.

Arriving at Cabo Gracias a Dios, the raiders, some 500 strong, proceeded upriver in canoes, leaving only small parties of men on board the ships. The expedition, however, proved abortive. The buccaneers had neglected to take along provisions in the expectation of capturing plentiful supplies along the route; but after travelling some fourteen days on the river without finding anything more than a few fruit trees along its banks, and spending several more days desperately searching through the forest and finding virtually nothing capable of sustaining life, they were reduced to eating even the shoes off their feet, and were compelled to return to the coast, as many of them were dying of hunger. It was not until they arrived among the Indians by the seashore that they were finally able to get some ordinary food.

With this episode, the final chapter on the evil Francis L'Olonnois and his crew was closed.

— Captain Henry Morgan —

Henry Morgan would have bitterly resented his inclusion in a book on pirates; and strictly speaking, he would have been quite correct. Throughout his seagoing career he had been a buccaneer, something of which he was proud to the end of his life. What sort of men, then, were the buccaneers?

The colonization of the West Indies by the English, the French, the Dutch and others in the 17th century brought with it a human flotsam and jetsam: men who tired of, or did not fit into colonial society and wanted independence and, they hoped, a life which would offer greater rewards. Many of these persons had come to the Caribbean as indentured servants, and finding themselves at a loose end when their indentures expired, they made their way to the island of Hispaniola, where, as has been explained in the chapter on Francis L'Olonnois, they lived by hunting wild cattle and pigs and smoke-drying the meat by a process called 'boucanning', before graduating, in due course, to piracy on the high seas.

Initially, these buccaneers were unorganised and operated in small groups; but when the English captured Jamaica in 1655 the buccaneers made Port Royal their base. By this time there may have been about 2,000 of them. The majority were English, many were French, and as in the case of the French Foreign Legion of a later era, men of any nationality were accepted into their ranks.

Although they made a living from piracy, the buccaneers differed from pirates in one important respect: they attacked the ships and settlements of Spain and sometimes of the

Henry Morgan

French and Dutch, but never of the English. Indeed, they claimed, with some justification, that everything they did was in furtherance of English interests and usually with official authority and support.

As his name suggests, Henry Morgan was a Welshman. We have it on the authority of a fellow buccaneer that he was at one time in Barbados, and it is generally accepted that he was the Henry Morgan, labourer, of Abergavenny, Monmouthshire, who sailed from Bristol in February 1656, bound for Barbados as an indentured servant. He was probably about 21 years of age. Nothing at all is known of his life in Barbados. Obviously he was of a restless disposition, and undoubtedly when his indenture expired, probably in 1660 or early in 1661, he decided to join the buccaneers and found his way to Jamaica.

Many buccaneering expeditions sailed from Jamaica in the years 1660-1665, most of them to Spanish possessions fringing the Caribbean. Henry Morgan must have been on many of them, but the first time he is mentioned by name is as one of the three leaders of a small expedition of a few hundred men, which in 1664 made successful attacks on the coast of Yucatan and followed this by a bold raid up the San Juan river into the heart of Nicaragua, capturing the capital city of Granada. The spoils of this expedition amounted to 50,000 pieces of eight, and Henry Morgan's reputation was well established.

When Charles II came to the throne in 1660 he hoped it would be possible to reach an accommodation with Spain, and the Governor of Jamaica was instructed to discontinue attacks on the Spanish in the Caribbean. For a few years, therefore, the activities of the buccaneers did not have official support, though no serious attempt was made to put a stop to them. In any case the Jamaica Governor had no force at his disposal to enable him to do so. By 1665 negotiations between England and Spain had broken down, and once again the Governor of Jamaica, Sir Thomas Modyford, used the buccaneers for attacks on Spanish settlements and shipping.

In 1665 the commander or 'admiral' of the buccaneers (who was, of course, elected by the buccaneers themselves) was a Dutchman known by his English name of Edward Mansfield. In June 1666, at Modyford's request, Mansfield, with Henry Morgan as his vice-admiral, sailed from Port Royal with 15 ships and some 500 men. Their objective was the island of Santa Catalina, or Providence, as it was called by the English. This island, which is not to be confused with New Providence in the Bahamas, lies off the coast of Central

America. It had originally been settled by the English, but it had been in Spanish hands since 1641.

It was Modyford's intention that Providence should again become an English possession, and he had already selected his own brother to be the Governor. When the defences had been strengthened the island would be an excellent springboard for expeditions against the Central and South American mainland. Providence was captured without difficulty, but the buccaneers reckoned that their job ended there. All they were interested in was booty, and once they had seized what was available they left. By the time Modyford was able to send a garrison and a Governor, the Spaniards had recaptured the island. The whole operation had been a waste of time, and Modyford had learnt a lesson.

Shortly after this, Mansfield disappears from the scene. There is some uncertainty about the circumstances, but it is believed that he fell into the hands of the Spaniards and was executed. The buccaneers appointed Henry Morgan to succeed him.

Morgan's first important expedition as commander was in 1668. At Modyford's request the expedition's first task was to be to make a reconnaissance of the south coast of Cuba to verify a rumour that the Spaniards were preparing to launch an attack from there on Jamaica. The expedition was then to attack Puerto Bello on the Isthmus of Panama, probably the largest port in Central America.

Morgan was not content with a reconnaissance, because this would yield no profit. The buccaneers were ordered to rendezvous near the mouth of the San Pedro River, and there he informed them that he intended to attack the town of Puerto del Principe, better known as Camaguey. This was well inland, and the Spaniards had always regarded it as immune from attack and had therefore made no provision for its defence.

Because of the distance which the buccaneers had to travel, the local governor did have some advance warning and he managed to assemble a force of about 800 men and to lay ambushes. These the buccaneers succeeded in avoiding, and in a pitched battle before the town the Spanish force was routed. On entering Puerto del Principe they encountered some further resistance from snipers, but this soon ceased when Morgan threatened to burn the town, together with its inhabitants. The buccaneers then proceeded to plunder the town, and having shut up the Spaniards in the church, they subjected them during the next few days to torture and starvation to force them to say where they had hidden their money and goods. They also went on marauding expeditions every day, bringing in fresh booty and more prisoners, and indulged themselves in orgies of feasting and drinking. Finally, when there was nothing more left to eat, drink, or plunder, they decided to leave.

Morgan had only moderate success in extorting a ransom in money from the population of Puerto del Principe in spite of his threat to reduce the town to ashes. As the amount forthcoming was less than he had hoped for, he finally settled for 500 head of cattle. These had to be driven down to the coast, where they were slaughtered and the meat salted and stowed on board the ships.

The spoils from the operations in Cuba, though far from paltry, had been less than had been hoped for; apart from silver plate and other valuables, they consisted of 50,000 pieces of eight. Morgan was looking to obtain a great deal more from his attack on Puerto Bello, but at this stage he suffered a setback. The French contingent decided that they had had enough and withdrew from the fleet, and it was only with difficulty that Morgan persuaded the English buccaneers to make the long voyage to Puerto Bello.

After Havana and Cartagena, Puerto Bello was the most fortified city in Spanish America. The attack on it was one of the most daring and hazardous that the buccaneers had ever undertaken, and it was of special importance to Morgan that it should succeed. The buccaneers judged their commander by results, and success on this occasion would greatly enhance Morgan's reputation.

Morgan's plan was to attack Puerto Bello from the land side, where the defences would be weakest. On the night of June 26th, 1668 the ships dropped anchor at Puerto del Pontin, about 12 miles west of Puerto Bello, and the buccaneers took to canoes and small rowing-boats, leaving only a sufficient number of men to man the ships and bring them into port next day. Finally, about midnight they landed at a place called Estero Longa Lemo and marched overland until they reached the city's first outpost. They had as guide an Englishman who had once been a prisoner in the country and knew the roads well; and a sentry they captured led them to a small fortified position on the city's outskirts, which they attacked and blew up together with its defenders when they failed to surrender.

The buccaneers then rushed into the sleeping city, and while some made for the convents and monasteries and took all the nuns and monks prisoner, others went on to attack the two forts. Under the personal command of the Governor, one of these forts put up so stubborn a resistance that the rovers failed to capture it even after several hours of fierce fighting; but when the other fort surrendered Morgan took fresh courage and resolved that he would take this one by any means and at all costs.

He finally resorted to a particularly fiendish stratagem. Convinced that the Spanish Governor would not order his men to fire upon other Spaniards, he had a dozen scaling ladders hastily constructed, each capable of enabling four men to climb at the same time. Then he ordered the monks and nuns who had been taken prisoner to carry the ladders, place them against the walls, and climb ahead of his men as human shields, while the buccaneers prodded them forward with their pikes and swords. But the Governor had no scruples about having his troops fire upon these harmless folk, and many of them were mowed down.

Morgan's cruel ruse proved effective, for his men succeeded in storming the walls of the fort and the Spaniards all surrendered, with the exception of the Governor himself,

Morgan at Puerto Bello

who would accept no quarter and accordingly met his death honourably on the field of battle.

With the defences of Puerto Bello now safely in their hands, Morgan's men proceeded to sack the city and, in customary fashion, the citizens were cruelly tortured to force them to reveal where their money and valuables were hidden. For about a fortnight the city was given up to riot and debauchery. An army taken by the President of Panama to relieve Puerto Bello was rudely beaten back by the battle-hardened buccaneers, who numbered only about 400, and finally the citizens were forced to raise the 100,000 pieces of eight Morgan had demanded of them as a ransom.

When the fleet returned to the rendezvous off Southern Cuba, it was found that the loot taken on the expedition amounted to some 215,000 pieces of eight in money, together with a large quantity of jewellery, silver plate, and other goods. And when the spoils had been shared out among the men Morgan returned to Jamaica loaded with wealth and personal prestige.

The main attraction of a buccaneering life was the great rewards that it offered. There was therefore keen competition to serve under a commander who had a successful record and Morgan had little difficulty in obtaining volunteers. But when, after perhaps months at sea and a series of hazardous engagements the expedition returned to port, the men like most such seafarers, wanted to enjoy themselves. Without thought for the morrow, they squandered their money in the notorious drinking and gambling dens of Port Royal, and not until their funds were exhausted could they be persuaded to go back to sea.

Towards the end of 1668 Morgan obtained a fresh commission from Governor Modyford to renew his attacks on Spanish settlements. The Isla de la Vaca, or Cow Island, off the southern coast of Hispaniola, was chosen as the rendezvous for the expedition, and it was there that in January 1669 the fleet assembled. At a meeting with his captains, Morgan decided to raid the villages in the region of

Caracas, Venezuela, but two incidents forced him to change his plans. First of all, the largest of his ships was blown up accidentally during a drunken party on board, and of the 300 Englishmen on board all except 30 lost their lives. Then, shortly afterwards, several of the captains changed their minds and withdrew from the fleet, which was now reduced to 8 ships and 500 men.

As a result of these setbacks, Morgan decided to attack the city of Maracaibo, situated on a lake of the same name. To this lake there was only narrow entrance. Probably to their surprise; certainly to their relief, the buccaneers were able to capture and dismantle the new fort commanding the entrance without undue difficulty. When they reached the city of Maracaibo itself, they found it deserted. Search parties brought in some booty from the neighbourhood, and also some prisoners, who as usual, were tortured to make them disclose where their goods and valuables were hidden. After three weeks in Maracaibo, the expedition moved to the large village of Gibraltar at the head of the lake and there they spent a profitable five weeks.

So far everything had gone smoothly, even if the loot had not come up to expectations, but when the fleet sailed down the lake to make their departure they found the exit blocked by three strongly armed Spanish ships. Morgan, ever resourceful, proved himself equal to the occasion. Loading one of his own vessels full of tar, pitch, sulphur and other combustibles, and adding several barrels of gunpowder with a slow-burning fuse, he lined the deck with dummy figures. With this vessel leading, the fleet moved towards the Spaniards.

The fireship with its skeleton crew made straight for the Spanish flagship, a vessel of 40 guns. It was only when they were grappled together that the Spanish commander realised that he was dealing with a floating bomb. He shouted to his men to go aboard her and get her free, but he was too late. Almost immediately there was a huge explosion; the flagship suffered some damage and was soon ablaze, and the crew had no option but to abandon her. The second Spanish ship ran aground while trying to seek the shelter of the fort, and the third was boarded and captured by the buccaneers.

This was not quite the end of the buccaneers' troubles. The fort was now strongly armed, and several attempts to storm it were repelled. Finally, at dusk, having suffered about 60 casualties, the buccaneers broke off the action, re-embarked and sailed for Jamaica. Though we do not know all the facts, it seems that the attack on the fort was unnecessary and could not have resulted in any material gain to the attackers. But it typified the spirit of the buccaneers, to whom any opposition presented a challenge which it was a matter of honour to meet.

For a while Henry Morgan retired to the large estate he had acquired in Jamaica, and settled down to enjoy his ill-gotten gains. Then in June 1670 came news that the Spanish governors in the Indies had received orders from home to make open war against the English; and when towards the end of that same month Jamaica's leeward coast was raided by the Spaniards, Governor Modyford at once commissioned Morgan Admiral and Commander-in-Chief of all the ships of war of Jamaica with full authority to attack the enemy at sea and on land.

On August 14th he sailed from Port Royal with 11 vessels and 600 men for the Isla de la Vaca, the rendezvous, where he was eventually joined by a large force of buccaneers from Tortuga and Hispaniola. There, at a conference held on December 2nd, he and all the captains resolved 'for the good of Jamaica and safety of us all' to attack and take the city of Panama.

The expedition consisting of 37 ships and some 2,000 fighting men, besides the sailors, set sail six days later, and in the middle of the month halted en route to capture once again the island of Santa Catalina. From there Morgan sent a detachment of nearly 500 men in advance to seize and hold the fortified town of Chagres on the Isthmus of Panama to open the way to Panama City.

When he arrived with his main force and found that the town had been secured, he appointed a garrison to hold it, and on January 9th, 1671 he set off up the Chagres River with 1,400 men in 7 ships and 36 boats. They were, however, obliged to disembark two days later, leaving 200 men behind to guard the vessels, and begin the long gruelling march overland to Panama through forest and swamp.

The buccaneers carried no food supplies, expecting to capture ample stocks on the way, but as they advanced they found that the Spaniards had carried off everything. Consequently, in addition to having to fight their way out of one ambush after another, they suffered severely from the pangs of hunger. But finally, on the ninth day of the march they came to a plain that was covered with cattle. At the sight of this vast quantity of meat on the hoof, the men at once broke ranks and shot down every animal within range.

After feasting on roasted meat to their hearts content they resumed their march towards their objective, which lay only a little farther away, and at the sight of the richest city of the Spanish Main the buccaneers broke into wild cheers. Then pitching camp on the plain, they beat their drums, blew their trumpets and waved their battle-flags in anticipation of victory the following day.

The next morning, January 18th, Morgan drew up his men in battle order to confront the powerful forces the Spaniards had raised to oppose him. Consisting mainly of some 2,100 infantry and 600 cavalry, the enemy, additionally, had assembled about 1,500 wild bulls which they intended driving into the rear ranks of the buccaneers to break up their formation.

The Spaniards attacked first with their cavalry, but when the horses got into marshy ground the floundering horsemen were almost wiped out by withering volleys from the ranks of the buccaneers. Then the Spanish infantry advanced, only to be promptly beaten back by the deadly marksmanship of these men who originally had been professional hunters. At this point the Spaniards drove the wild bulls

Morgan at Panama

forward, but the buccaneers stood their ground and poured volleys of musketry into the charging animals, which took fright and scattered in all directions. Scores of them turned back and stampeded into the ranks of the Spanish infantry. In this battle, which lasted two hours, the Spaniards were finally routed, leaving an estimated 600 men dead on the field, in addition to the wounded.

After they had rested, the buccaneers advanced on the city. They were surprised to find the streets barricaded and defended by batteries of cannon, but they overcame all opposition and in two hours the city was in their hands. The freebooters then embarked upon an orgy of looting, killing, and torturing that is still regarded as one of history's greatest atrocities. Then Panama was set on fire, allegedly by the buccaneers, though Morgan claimed by the Spaniards themselves, and burnt almost entirely to the ground.

When he and his men finally left the ruined city after a stay of 28 days, they carried away 175 mules laden with money, silver, and other valuable merchandise, besides several hundred prisoners, whom Morgan held to ransom. He was totally unmoved by the distress of these helpless folk, who included many infants and young children, and told them quite plainly that he had not come to listen to their groans but to get money, and 'they would never get out of his clutches without it.'

Master schemer as he was, it appears that Morgan had formed a plan to cheat his men of their fair share of the plunder, and when the booty was distributed on their return to Chagres each man received no more than 200 pieces of eight. This naturally caused considerable discontent, but Morgan ignored all complaints. One morning the rovers awoke to find that he had got secretly on board his own ship and sailed off back to Jamaica, followed by three or four vessels belonging to his closest friends who, apparently, had been more substantially rewarded for their part in the enterprise.

On May 31st, 1671 Henry Morgan received the formal

thanks of Governor Modyford and the Council of Jamaica. But it happened that in the same week the Governor had commissioned him to take hostile action against the Spaniards a treaty was being concluded, unknown to both men, between England and Spain.

That summer Sir Thomas Modyford was sent home, a prisoner, to answer for having issued a commission against the Spaniards after the treaty had been signed; and early the next year his successor, Sir Thomas Lynch, similarly sent Morgan to England to answer for his attacks on a nation with which England was at peace. But his disgrace proved short, for in 1674, only two years later, mainly on account of a deterioration in Anglo-Spanish relations, Morgan was reportedly in high favour with his Sovereign, Charles II, who knighted him that same year and sent him back to Jamaica with a commission as Lieutenant-Governor.

In the succeeding years the ex-buccaneer remained in the Colony, taking an active part in public administration, attending church regularly and, ironically, suppressing buccaneering and piracy with a heavy hand. On August 25th, 1688 he died, and the next day he was buried near Gallows Point, Port Royal, where he had hanged so many of his former associates during the past few years. Less than four years later, on June 7th, 1692, Port Royal, which had the reputation of being the most wicked city in the western hemisphere, was destroyed and submerged beneath the sea by one of the greatest earthquakes ever recorded, and the tomb of Henry Morgan disappeared together with everything else.

The cruelty and ruthlessness he frequently exercised, or permitted, during his buccaneering career have left an indelible blot upon his reputation, as has his dishonesty in the distribution of the spoils among his followers. There can be little doubt that the various sums he shared out after the sack of Puerto Bello, Maracaibo, Panama, and other places on the Spanish Main represented only a small proportion of the great harvest of plunder taken.

Captain Benjamin Hornigold
The Pirate Who Reformed

'A nest of pirates are endeavouring to establish themselves in New Providence,' reported Governor Alexander Spotswood of Virginia to the Council of Trade and Plantations in London in July 1716.

This report was well founded, but was nothing new, for in April 1714, more than two years earlier, Lieutenant Governor Pulleine of Bermuda had written informing the Council that New Providence, as well as two other islands in the Bahamas, had lately become a retreat for pirates. There were three sets of them, he stated, and they were committing their depredations in open boats, with about 25 men in a boat, and within the past eight months they had robbed the Spaniards of booty valued £60,000.

By 1715, Benjamin Hornigold, named as one of their captains, was in possession of a sloop equipped with 10 guns and a crew of 135 men, and with a certain Captain Thomas Barrow and certain others was engaged in attacking and plundering ships of every nationality, from the Bahamas to the North American seaboard.

Soon the Bahamas became a mart at which large quantities of piratical goods were openly sold and bought, and the pirates there became so powerful and insolent that in June 1716 no less distinguished a person than the Chief Justice of New Providence, Thomas Walker, was forced to flee with his family to South Carolina after Benjamin Hornigold had threatened to murder him.

A little later, Hornigold's ship was taken and destroyed by vessels commissioned by Governor Robert Johnson of South

Carolina, but he himself escaped, and it was not long before he was again operating out of New Providence.

Some time late in that year, 1716, a certain Edward Teach, a man destined to greatly exceed him in infamy, took ship with Hornigold, apparently as mate, and was soon given command of a sloop they took as a prize.

Early in 1717 Hornigold in his sloop of 10 guns and a crew of 80 men, and Teach in the other with six guns and about 70 men sailed together out of New Providence for a cruise off the North American mainland, and after taking and plundering at least three vessels en route they put into a secluded cove on the coast of Virginia to careen and clean their ships.

This task would have involved moving the vessels as close as possible to the shore at high tide, and as the tide receded, heaving them over on their sides by means of block and tackle attached to stout trees on the shore and having all hands scrape the barnacles from their bottoms and put on a coat of tallow while the tide was still out. Afterwards, the vessels would have been righted and refloated on an incoming tide.

After this task was completed the two pirate captains sailed again for the Caribbean, and in the latitude of the Bahamas captured a large French ship. Hornigold put Teach on board as her captain and returned alone to New Providence.

When Woodes Rogers arrived there in July 1718 as Governor of the Bahamas, Captain Hornigold was one of several pirates who formed themselves into a ludicrous guard of honour to receive him, and immediately took advantage of the Royal pardon Rogers had been empowered to grant to all those who surrendered by the date stipulated.

Just under two months later Hornigold was back at sea; but this time in the service of law and order.

It happened that on the arrival of Governor Rogers, the leader of the pirate community, Captain Charles Vane, refused to surrender unconditionally and accept the King's pardon, but put to sea instead, flying his black flag in a gesture of defiance.

Two vessels sent in pursuit failed to catch up with him, but in the middle of September word reached the Governor that Vane's sloop, together with two prizes he had taken, was anchored at Green Turtle Cay, near the island of Abaco. As the three naval vessels that had accompanied the Governor to New Providence had since left, Rogers armed and equipped a sloop and perhaps on the principle, 'set a thief to catch a thief', placed Hornigold, the ex-pirate in command with orders to proceed to Green Turtle Cay, make a reconnaisance, and return and make a report on Vane's activities.

When several days passed and he did not return, the Governor and everyone else concluded that he had gone off and resumed his old career. But actually, from a well-concealed position, Hornigold had been keeping Vane under close observation in the hope of taking him or some of his

Woodes Rogers with his son and daughter outside Fort Nassau. This picture was painted by William Hogarth in 1729.

finally returned to New Providence after three weeks absence, he brought in a sloop the Governor had granted permission to go turtle-fishing, but which was discovered trading with the pirates. Governor Rogers seized this vessel and promptly had her captain thrown into prison, and now became convinced that the ex-pirate had sincerely reformed and had really abandoned his evil ways.

It was about this time that on account of a scarcity of provisions and livestock at New Providence the Governor decided to establish some trade with certain merchants in Cuba, and on October 15th, 1718 he despatched three vessels from New Providence laden with cargoes of goods and merchandise. The very next day, however, several of the sailors who previously had been pirates and had not long before received the King's pardon, armed themselves and treacherously seized control of the vessels. They then set about maltreating everyone who refused to join them and marooned them on an uninhabited island.

A few days later, however, three Spanish privateers happened to call at the island and discovered the castaways, and the Spaniards gave them a large sail-boat, which enabled them to make their way back to New Providence.

Governor Rogers immediately commissioned Benjamin Hornigold to go and seek out the band of relapsed marauders and bring them in. He finally caught up with them on November 15th and returned with 10 prisoners.

On December 9th and 10th a special Court of Admiralty Sessions, comprising the Governor and seven assistants, who included two former pirate captains, was held at Nassau for the trial of the prisoners. Judgement on one of them was postponed until a later date, for some reason, but the others were found guilty and sentenced to death.

At ten o'clock on the morning of December 12th the condemned pirates were escorted to the place of execution, where they spent 45 minutes beneath the gallows joining in the recital of prayers and the singing of psalms and in addressing exhortations to the crowd, who included many of their former associates. Immediately before he ordered the Provost Marshal to proceed with the hanging, the Governor reprieved one man he considered deserving of mercy; then, at the Provost Marshal's command, the hangman hauled away the three large casks supporting the platform on which the men stood, and in a trice the prisoners were suspended in space.

In a letter to Secretary of State, James Craggs, in London a fortnight later, Governor Woodes Rogers gave the ex-pirate full credit for the part he had played in bringing this criminal gang to justice. 'I am glad,' he stated, 'of this new proof Captain Hornigold has given the world to wipe off the infamous name he has hitherto been known by, tho' in the very acts of piracy he committed most people spoke well of his generosity.'

Although war between Britain and Spain broke out afresh that same December and the threat of a Spanish invasion was soon looming over the Bahamas, Governor Rogers continued his relentless campaign to rid the Bahamas of pirates. By 1721, when he returned to England, he had succeeded largely on account of the efficiency of Captain Benjamin Hornigold in hunting down his former associates. The reformed sea-rover thereafter fades from history, and nothing appears to be known as to how, when, or where he ended his days.

Edward Teach, alias Blackbeard

Edward Teach, generally regarded as the most ferocious pirate of all time, was reputed to have been born in Bristol, England, and to have served in privateers that operated out of Jamaica during the War of the Spanish Succession (1702-1713), in America called 'Queen Anne's War'; but it is not known when he actually joined the fighting.

It is said that he frequently distinguished himself by his personal bravery in action, but nonetheless was never appointed to command any vessel of his own until after he had taken up a career of piracy about the end of 1716, serving under the notorious Captain Benjamin Hornigold. It appears that on one occasion when the latter captured a trading sloop he fitted it out as a pirate vessel and installed Teach as captain. The two men then sailed together out of New Providence in the Bahamas, which at that time was the pirate haven of the New World.

While on a voyage to the American mainland Teach and Hornigold captured a ship bound out of Havana, Cuba, with a cargo of flour. A second vessel out of Bermuda was taken later, and after they had relieved her of a large quantity of wine the pirates let her go. Finally they captured a ship travelling to South Carolina out of Madeira and were delighted to discover that she was carrying a cargo of considerable value.

The latter part of the year found Teach and Hornigold in the West Indies, and one day, near St Vincent, they seized the *Concord*, a large French ship bound from Guinea, West Africa, to Martinique with a cargo consisting of slaves, gold

Edward Teach (A General History of the Pirates *Daniel Defoe, 1724)*

dust, plate, and other valuables. After the pirates had thoroughly plundered this vessel Hornigold put Teach on board as her captain and then returned alone to New Providence, where, on the arrival of Governor Woodes Rogers in July 1718, he surrendered and received the King's pardon, and shortly afterwards entered the Governor's service as a hunter of pirates.

As Teach was now completely free to sail on his own he had reached the turning point in his career. He lost no time in arming his new ship with some 40 guns and then changed her name to the *Queen Anne's Revenge*. This was a name that before long would strike fear into the heart of every peaceable mariner in the New World.

It would appear that it was not long after he had taken command of the *Queen Anne's Revenge* that while cruising again near St Vincent, Teach sighted a large merchant ship. She turned out to be the *Great Allen*, commanded by Captain Christopher Taylor, on her way from Barbados to Jamaica with a valuable cargo. The pirates plundered her of whatever they fancied, including a fine silver cup, and severely maltreated her captain. Then after putting all the men ashore, they set the ship on fire and sank her.

A few days later Teach encountered *HMS Scarborough*, a British man-of-war armed with 30 guns, but severely undermanned, commanded by Captain Hume, sent out from Barbados to seek out and destroy the *Queen Anne's Revenge*. After a running battle that lasted several hours, the pirates' superiority in armament finally prevailed, and the *Scarborough* was forced to withdraw, badly damaged, and return to her station at Barbados. Teach did not think it worthwhile to pursue a ship that carried no cargo. The fact that he had met one of the King's ships in battle and defeated her was of much greater value to him since it served to boost his reputation as a bold and fearless pirate leader.

It was, perhaps, about this time that Edward Teach became convinced that his prospects of achieving success on the high seas would be greatly improved if he adopted a physical appearance that would inspire fear in his victims. At that period very few men wore beards, so he cultivated an enormous jet-black beard, which he habitually braided into pigtails and tied with ribbons. This not only soon earned him the nickname 'Blackbeard' by which he became better known; it also became, as he had intended, a symbol of terror from the Caribbean Sea to the seaboard of New England.

In preparing himself for action Teach would wear across his shoulders a sling in which were fixed several pistols;

while in a broad belt around his waist would be an assortment of daggers and pistols as well as a huge cutlass. Then, as a finishing touch, he would tuck several fuses under the brim of his hat. These consisted of thick hemp cord that had been dipped in a special solution which caused them to burn slowly, and were the same as those used to touch off the ship's cannons. When he set these alight the wisps of smoke around his face added a demonic aspect to his already fearsome appearance. It is hardly surprising that the crew of many a merchant ship would surrender without offering the slightest resistance on encountering the *Queen Anne's Revenge* and descrying this satanic figure standing menacingly on her deck.

Apparently, it was not long after Blackbeard's fight with *HMS Scarborough* that he met with another pirate vessel at sea. She was the *Revenge*, a sloop armed with ten guns and manned by a crew of some 70 hands under the command of one Major Stede Bonnet, a wealthy Barbadian planter, who not long before had taken to the career of a sea rover. After some discussion, the two men, one a professional, the other an amateur, agreed to sail in partnership, and for some time operated together in the Eastern Caribbean plundering shipping and, on one occasion, even raiding and burning a settlement on the French island of Guadeloupe.

In a despatch dated early January 1718 sent to the Council of Trade and Plantations in London, the Governor of the Leeward Islands, William Hamilton, reported how, the previous November, Teach and Bonnet had taken several trading sloops belonging to the island of St Christopher and had also sunk a ship laden with sugar they had captured off Guadeloupe. Among a number of documents annexed to this despatch was the deposition of Henry Bostock, Master of the sloop *Margaret* of St Christopher, who stated that on December 5th, while off Crab Island, he met the two pirate vessels and Teach took his cargo of cattle and hogs as well as his arms, books, and instruments. The pirates did not maltreat him, he added, but they forced two members of his crew to join them, and one other man joined them voluntarily.

Though Major Bonnet had taken an active part in all these operations, Blackbeard had become all too aware that he was totally lacking in any knowledge and experience of seamanship. Accordingly he persuaded Bonnet to turn the command of his sloop, the *Revenge*, over to a certain Richards, one of his (Blackbeard's) men and take a cabin on board the *Queen Anne's Revenge*, where, he assured him, he would be free of the rigours and responsibilities of commanding a ship and would be able to lead a leisurely life.

The two pirate ships were on a voyage to the Bay of Honduras, when they stopped to take on a supply of water at Turneffe, off the coast of what is now called Belize. While they were at anchor there, a trading sloop entered the harbour, totally unsuspecting of any danger, and immediately Richards raised anchor and headed for the vessel, which speedily surrendered on sighting the black flags of the pirate.

She was the *Adventure*, just arrived from Jamaica, and Teach took her captain, David Harriot, and her crew on board the *Queen Anne's Revenge*, where they all readily agreed to join the pirates. He then sent Israel Hands, the sailing master of the *Queen Anne's Revenge*, with a party of men to take charge of the prize.

After about a week's stay at Turneffe the pirates, on April 9th, resumed the voyage to the Bay of Honduras, where they found four sloops at anchor as well as a larger ship called the *Protestant Caesar*, commanded by a Captain Wyar. No sooner had Blackbeard hoisted his black flag and fired a warning shot than Captain Wyar and his crew took to their boats and fled ashore. Blackbeard's quartermaster, William Howard, and eight men then boarded the ship, and after looting her they set her on fire on discovering that she belonged to Boston, Massachusetts, where, the previous October, the authorities had hanged a batch of pirates. The pirates also spitefully burned one of the sloops, but allowed the other three to go free after plundering them of everything of value.

From the Bay of Honduras the whole company then sailed to Grand Cayman, an island about 200 miles WNW of Jamaica, where they took a small vessel engaged in catching turtles, and then made for the Bahamas, where they occupied themselves for a short while in hunting for treasure in the hulls of the numerous ships wrecked on the rocky islets.

Blackbeard's squadron, which now consisted of five vessels altogether, afterwards sailed for South Carolina and arrived outside the entrance to the harbour at Charles Town (now Charleston) some time late in May. Immediately they set up a blockade of the port, seizing all vessels entering and leaving - the first to be taken being the pilot boat. Next was a large ship, the *Crowley*, commanded by Captain Robert Clark, which was headed for London with a number of prominent persons on board, including a certain Samuel Wragg, a member of the Council of South Carolina.

It happened that Blackbeard by this time had run desperately short of medicines and decided that he would demand a substantial quantity from the authorities at Charles Town. With these passengers held as hostages he was placed in a very favourable bargaining position, and accordingly, he sent one of them ashore accompanied by four of his men including Richards, the captain of the *Revenge*, with a message threatening the Council that if they did not provide him immediately with a chest of medicines and allow his men to return unharmed he would have all the prisoners killed and their heads sent in to the Governor, and would also burn the ships he had captured.

While Mr Marks, the prisoner, was in conference with the Council, Richards and his three companions strode arrogantly about the streets of the town. The citizens were irate at the boldness of these men whom they regarded as robbers and murderers, but no one dared lay hands on them. The Council, quite naturally concerned that the prisoners should not be harmed, agreed to Blackbeard's demands and sent on board a large chest containing between £300 and £400 worth of medicines. Blackbeard then released the ships and the prisoners, but not before he had robbed them of about £1,500 in gold and pieces of eight, besides provisions and other goods. He then departed with his squadron for North Carolina.

For some time he had been planning to disband the company, and had carefully devised a scheme to secure all the money and booty for himself and his favourite henchmen and cheat the others. On arriving on the coast of North Carolina, where he intended to put his scheme into execution, he ordered his vessels into Topsail Inlet (today called Beaufort Inlet) on the pretext of having them careened and cleaned, and when the *Queen Anne's Revenge* entered the inlet he deliberately ran her aground on a sand-bar.

Pretending this to be an accident, he immediately called on Israel Hands for assistance in getting her off. Hands, who was fully aware of his chief's intentions, had lines thrown from two of the sloops, and while pretending to extricate the ship he contrived to run them aground as well so that they too were lost and only the *Adventure* and the *Revenge* now remained.

The first phase of Blackbeard's plan had gone well, and with 40 of his men he transferred to the *Adventure*. He restored Bonnet to the command of his sloop, the *Revenge*, and announced his intention of proceeding to Bath Town (now Bath) to surrender and receive the pardon King George I had proclaimed for all pirates who should surrender by September 5th – a time-limit later extended by four months.

Bonnet similarly decided to take advantage of this amnesty and made his way overland to Bath Town, where he was given a certificate of pardon. But when he returned to Topsail Inlet he found that Blackbeard had absconded with all the money and the plunder the company had accumulated. He was also soon to be informed that Blackbeard, in accordance with his scheme to reduce the number of those entitled to share in the spoils, had also put 25 of his men ashore on a small barren island that contained nothing capable of providing shelter or sustaining life.

Bonnet went and rescued these men from the lingering death that would certainly have been theirs, and then sailed in pursuit of Blackbeard. But he never saw him again.

On arriving at Bath Town with about 20 men, the remnant of his crew, Teach surrendered to Charles Eden, the Governor of North Carolina, and received his certificate. Curiously enough the two men soon became very friendly, and the first favour the Governor granted the pirate was to give him a legal right to his sloop, the *Adventure*, which he had piratically taken at Turneffe when he was operating in the *Queen Anne's Revenge*. This was accomplished simply by holding a Court of Vice-Admiralty and condemning the vessel as a privateer's prize taken from the Spaniards although, in fact, England and Spain were actually at peace at the time and the vessel had actually been captured from British subjects.

Shortly after this Blackbeard got married, allegedly for the fourteenth time, and settled down to life on land. But only briefly, for like so many who had accepted the King's pardon, he relapsed into his old ways and was soon back at sea.

Off Bermuda he met and plundered two or three English ships and then captured two French vessels. One of the latter happened to be carrying very little cargo, but the other, en route to France from Martinique, was loaded with sugar and cocoa. After transferring her crew to the lightly laden vessel, Blackbeard took her to Ocracoke Inlet, back in North Carolina, where he and some of his crew made sworn declarations to the Authorities that they had found her abandoned at sea with no one on board.

Once more Governor Eden called a Court of Vice-Admiralty, which condemned the ship; and her cargo was then divided among the Governor, the Secretary of the Province, and the pirates.

Blackbeard however soon became disturbed over the possibility that some mariner coming into the anchorage might recognise the French vessel and disclose the truth to the Authorities, so, pretending that she was leaky and unseaworthy, he obtained Governor Eden's permission to sink her, and then moved her into the deeper water of the Pamticoe River and set her on fire.

Blackbeard did not return to the high seas after this, but instead took to plundering the numerous small vessels that traded up and down the river. The traders and planters were anxious to have an end put to these robberies but had become firmly convinced that no action could be expected from their own Governor, Charles Eden. They therefore sent a delegation secretly to neighbouring Virginia to seek aid from the Lieutenant Governor, Alexander Spotswood, who was noted not only for his stern opposition to piracy but who also shared their lack of confidence in the integrity of the Government of North Carolina.

Governor Spotswood readily agreed to send a force to destroy Blackbeard, and after consulting with the commanders of the two guard-ships from the Royal Navy, the *Pearl* and the *Lyme*, which for some months past had been anchored in the James River, he hired two sloops with pilots and had them equipped with ammunition and small arms, but no cannon. These vessels, manned by 54 men from the men-of-war and commanded by Lieutenant Maynard of the *Pearl* and Mr Hyde of the *Lyme* finally sailed south on November 17th in search of Blackbeard and his crew.

At the same time that the preparations were being made for this expedition, Governor Spotswood had the Provincial Assembly enact a statute 'to encourage the apprehending and destroying of pyrates'. This authorised rewards to be paid for the killing of pirates in general, with the largest reward of £100 to be paid for the killing specifically of 'Edward Teach, commonly called Captain Teach, or Blackbeard'.

The armed sloops finally caught up with him on

45

November 22nd at his favourite anchorage at Ocracoke Inlet, North Carolina. He was on board the *Adventure*, which carried eight guns and was altogether well equipped for fighting, and when he realised that the vessels approaching were manned by men of the King's navy he seized a great bowl of rum and shouted to the officers:

'Damnation to anyone who should give or ask quarter.'

Lieutenant Maynard shouted back:

'I expect no quarter from you and shall give none.'

Blackbeard then drank off the bowl of liquor in a single draught and opened fire on the sloops. His cannon, loaded with small shot, immediately killed and wounded some 20 of the naval men, whose vessels afforded no protective cover.

Maynard's strategy was not to board the pirates but rather to lure them on to his own ship, where he had most of his men lying in ambush below deck. As his sloop drew alongside the *Adventure* the pirates hurled a number of grenades on to his deck. These were bottles filled with powder, small shot, and pieces of metal, and ignited with fuses, and were usually very effective in causing injury and confusion. Blackbeard and his men then leapt on board Maynard's sloop, and at Maynard's signal the men concealed below rushed up on deck and engaged the pirates in a deadly hand-to-hand struggle.

Finally the two leaders came face to face and attacked first with pistols; then with swords. But unluckily Maynard's sword was soon broken by a powerful blow from Black-beard's cutlass. As Maynard stepped backward to cock his pistol the pirate moved in for the kill, but at that instant a seaman delivered him a slashing blow across the face. Maynard fired a ball into him, but still Blackbeard stood his ground. The bloody contest continued and the Lieutenant fired again just as another of his men, wielding a broad-sword, delivered a deadly blow to the pirate's neck. Still Blackbeard kept his feet; but he was weakening from loss of blood, and just as he was cocking his pistol he fell dead on to the blood-soaked deck, his body covered in 25 wounds.

The fight between Lieutenant Maynard and Blackbeard (The
Pirates' Own Book *1842)*

When the surviving pirates saw their leader slain they
jumped overboard and called out for quarter, which was
granted. Lieutenant Maynard then had Blackbeard's head
cut off, and he returned to Virginia to claim his reward with
this ghastly trophy suspended from the bowsprit of his sloop.

Accounts differ as to the number of casualties sustained in
this action; but Governor Spotswood of Virginia reported to

London that Blackbeard and nine of his men were killed and nine taken prisoner, though all the latter were wounded. And of the King's men 10 were killed and 24 wounded - one of whom died later.

The surviving members of Blackbeard's crew, taken to Virginia, were put on trial the following March, and all except one were found guilty and sentenced to death by hanging.

Thus was closed the final chapter on the life and career of Edward Teach, alias Blackbeard, the terror of the Caribbean and the Carolinas - a man whose name is still synonymous with piracy after more than two and a half centuries.

Stede Bonnet, Gentleman Pirate

Of the numerous sea rovers who infested the Caribbean Sea and the Atlantic seaboard of North America during the so-called 'golden age of piracy', none had less cause to take up that career than Major Stede Bonnet.

The Major was born in 1688 in Barbados, the eldest of the three children of a prosperous planter, Edward Bonnet, and Sarah his wife, and on the death of his father in 1695 he inherited a substantial estate. As his mother did not long survive his father Stede and his two sisters were brought up by guardians, who saw to it that they received a good upbringing and education in accordance with the wishes expressed in their father's will.

Shortly after reaching his majority in 1709, Stede Bonnet married the eldest daughter of another planter, William Allamby, by whom he subsequently had three sons and a daughter, and took up residence in the Bay district, just outside the centre of Bridgetown, the seaside capital of Barbados.

Bonnet's substantial holding in land qualified him for the rank of major in the island's militia. He involved himself in public affairs and altogether became so exemplary a citizen he was appointed a Justice of the Peace and sworn in on January 24th, 1716.

With this kind of background it will be observed that Major Stede Bonnet was not the kind of individual likely to take up a career in crime; yet this was precisely what he did.

Early in the year 1717 he bought himself a sloop, armed it with ten guns, and recruited a pirate crew of 70 men from

Stede Bonnet

around the Bridgetown waterfront. He named this vessel the *Revenge*, a name much in vogue among pirate fleets of that period.

It would appear that Bonnet made all these preparations discreetly, pretending that he was going abroad on some business or trading venture, because on March 25th, before he sailed, he had a legal document carefully drawn up granting his wife and two of his friends power to act during his absence as his attorneys in all matters appertaining to his personal and business affairs.

Everyone who was acquainted with the Major must therefore have been greatly shocked when news eventually reached Barbados that the business upon which he had actually embarked was piracy on the high seas. Some of his friends charitably attributed this crime to a certain mental imbalance they asserted they had observed in him for some time. Some others, again, were of the opinion that marital troubles had driven him to that extreme. On the other hand, he may have taken to the seas merely out of a craving for excitement. But whatever the reason, Major Bonnet was far from being qualified for the career he had taken up, for he was totally ignorant of seamanship.

Despite this serious handicap his first cruise was amazingly successful. This was off the Capes of Virginia, where he took several ships and plundered them of provisions, money, and other valuables. One of these vessels, the *Turbet*, of his native Barbados, he burned after putting her crew ashore. Undoubtedly, this was to prevent news of his activities from being taken back to the island.

Bonnet and his crew then sailed for the coast of New York, and after taking and plundering a sloop off the eastern end of Long Island, they went to nearby Gardiner's Island and took on a stock of provisions and, surprisingly, actually paid for them.

After operating for some time in this area Bonnet sailed for South Carolina and in August 1717 arrived off the Bar of Charles Town (now Charleston), where he captured two incoming vessels: one of them a New England brigantine; the other a sloop belonging to Barbados loaded with rum, sugar, and slaves. Bonnet released the former after relieving her of her cargo, but he and his men carried off the Barbados sloop to a secluded inlet in North Carolina and occupied her while they careened and cleaned the *Revenge*. When this task was completed they set the sloop on fire and sank her.

After this, Bonnet's crew were undecided about where to go for their next cruise. Some favoured one destination while others preferred another, and Bonnet's inexperience in all matters appertaining to the sea placed him at a disadvantage in his dealings with these hardened seafarers.

It however appears that a decision was finally made to sail to the Caribbean, where he encountered the notorious Edward Teach, better known as Blackbeard, and entered into partnership with him, assuming the name of Edwards. An account of Bonnet's activities and adventures in the West Indies and elsewhere as a member of Blackbeard's company has already been given in the story of Blackbeard and need not be repeated here.

About the time he surrendered himself to the authorities at Bath Town (now Bath), North Carolina, and received his certificate of pardon for his past acts of piracy, it happened that war broke out in Europe between Spain and the Triple Alliance comprising England, France, and Holland, and Bonnet, now restored by Blackbeard to the command of his sloop, the *Revenge*, obtained a clearance to proceed to the island of St Thomas to secure a privateer's commission to operate against the Spaniards. His crew readily agreed to serve with him in this enterprise, but just as he was preparing to sail from Topsail Inlet word reached him that Blackbeard's ship, the *Adventure*, was lying at anchor at Ocracoke Inlet a few miles away, with about 20 hands on board.

Anxious to settle some old scores for insults his former partner had showered upon him, and also for having finally cheated him of his share of the booty, Bonnet immediately sailed in pursuit, but he arrived to find that Blackbeard had gone. After cruising four days searching for him without any success, Bonnet set course for Virginia, having now abandoned any intention of going to St Thomas.

July of 1718 found him and his crew operating again off the Capes of Virginia, the scene of his earliest adventures, and the first vessel they encountered was carrying a cargo of supplies they needed badly. The pirates took several barrels of pork and a substantial quantity of bread; but they didn't intend this to be an act of piracy and accordingly gave in exchange several casks of rice and an old cable.

A couple of days later, near Cape Henry, they chased and captured a sloop which they were delighted to find laden with several hogsheads of rum and molasses. After relieving her of a few of these, Bonner put eight of his men in charge of the vessel; but soon afterwards they absconded with her and were never seen again.

After this, the Major abandoned all restraint. He had received his pardon under his own name, Bonnet, and now assuming the name Captain Thomas and renaming his sloop the *Royal James*, he hoisted his piratical 'Bloody Flag' and relapsed in earnest into his old career, ruthlessly plundering every vessel he encountered in the coastal waters of Virginia. From there, he and his crew then sailed to the vicinity of Philadelphia, taking, en route, at least four vessels which they plundered and then released.

Then on July 2nd, off Delaware Bay, Major Bonnet, alias Captain Thomas, took a sloop outbound from Philadelphia to his native island, Barbados, with a cargo of provisions. He kept this vessel and put a small party of his men on board. Two days later he captured and similarly kept the merchant sloop, *Frances*, commanded by Captain Peter Manwaring, inbound to Philadelphia from Antigua with a valuable cargo consisting mainly of rum, molasses, sugar, cotton, and indigo.

By this time the *Royal James* had become rather leaky, and Bonnet decided to take her, together with his two prizes, to the Cape Fear River to have repairs carried out. This task occupied the pirates for six weeks, and the delay proved to be the undoing of Bonnet and his entire crew, for a report of their presence eventually reached the ears of the authorities at Charles Town.

The South Carolina Council were alarmed at this news,

fearing a repetition of the events of the previous May, when Blackbeard had blockaded the port, seized several ships and held their crews and passengers captive, and had blackmailed the Council into providing him with a chest of medical supplies.

But this time Colonel William Rhett, a distinguished citizen of the province, approached Governor Robert Johnson and requested a commission to take two armed sloops to the Cape Fear River and attack the pirates. The Governor issued the commission, and in a few days two sloops were equipped and manned - the *Henry* with 8 guns and 70 men, under Captain John Masters, and the *Sea Nymph* with 8 guns and 60 men, under Captain Fayrer Hall, but with Colonel Rhett, as commander of the expedition.

On September 14th two vessels crossed the harbour to Sullivan's Island, where the final preparations were made; but just as the expedition was about to sail, Rhett's plan was disrupted by a startling piece of news. A small vessel from Antigua came into port and reported how, a few days before, she had been taken just off the bar and plundered by the pirate, Charles Vane, in a brigantine of 12 guns and 90 men, and that Vane had also taken two other vessels and then spent some time cruising in the area hunting for further prey.

On being further informed that the pirates were heard saying that they intended going southward, Rhett took his sloops in that direction and searched for Vane in the rivers and creeks, but having failed to find him he changed course and sailed on his original mission to the Cape Fear River.

On the evening of the 26th of the month he entered the river and saw three sloops at anchor. These were Bonnet's *Royal James* and her two prizes. But it appears that the Colonel's pilot was unfamiliar with the channel and soon ran both his vessels aground. When they were finally refloated it was too dark for them to proceed up river and they were obliged to anchor for the night.

When Bonnet, or Captain Thomas, as he still called

himself, noticed the two sloops anchored down-river he thought they were defenceless merchant vessels and sent off a party of men in three boats to board and capture them. But it did not take the pirates long to discover with what manner of craft they had to deal, and they hastened back to their chief with the unwelcome news.

Stede Bonnet realised that the following day would bring a desperate struggle, so he recalled all the men he had put on board the two prizes and set all hands to work during the night preparing the *Royal James* for action. He also took some time to write a letter, addressed to Governor Johnson, which he showed to Captain Manwaring, one of his prisoners. This letter threatened that if he succeeded in escaping from the two vessels the Governor had sent against him he would burn and destroy every ship entering or leaving South Carolina.

The next morning the *Royal James* got under way and went down-stream intending to fight her way past the enemy and get out to the open sea. Colonel Rhett's sloops immediately gave chase and attempted to get on either side of her, but in the heat of the action all caution was forgotten and all three vessels entered shoal water and ran aground. The *Henry*, with Colonel Rhett on board, found herself listing in a position that exposed her deck to the merciless fire of the pirates, who all the while also amused themselves shouting taunts at her crew. She nonetheless returned their fire for nearly five hours until a rising tide finally freed her from her dangerous situation.

After her crew had moved her into deeper water and repaired her rigging, she returned to finish off the *Royal James*, which still remained grounded, whereupon, the pirates seeing that their situation was now hopeless, speedily surrendered and were taken prisoner.

Colonel Rhett was delighted to discover that Captain Thomas, their leader, was in reality none other than the notorious Major Stede Bonnet, whose name was infamous from the Caribbean Sea to the New England seaboard; a man who had not only taken and plundered numerous ships up and down the Carolina coast but had also taken part in the infamous blockade of the port of Charles Town.

The casualties suffered by the Colonel's expedition were 12 men killed and 18 wounded. The pirates, on the other hand, had 7 men killed and 5 wounded, 2 of them mortally.

Colonel Rhett departed with his ships from the Cape Fear River on September 30th and arrived back at Charles Town on October 3rd to the acclaim of a jubilant population. Two days later the prisoners were put ashore, and as the town then had no prison Bonnet's men were lodged in the watchhouse under a guard provided by the militia, while he himself, in deference to his social background as a gentleman by birth, was committed into the custody of the Provost-Marshal, Captain Nathaniel Partridge, at his residence.

A few days later he was joined there by David Harriot, the sailing master of the *Royal James*, and Ignatius Pell, the boatswain, both of whom had been removed from the watchhouse after they had agreed to testify for the Crown against their fellow pirates.

Although two sentries were posted at the Provost-Marshal's house every night, Bonnet and Harriot nonetheless managed to escape custody on October 24th. The boatswain in fact refused to go along with them. The escape of the two men caused a considerable uproar among the population of Charles Town, who openly voiced their suspicions that the authorities had somehow connived at the escape. But more than likely it was the Provost-Marshal himself who was the guilty party. Like Bonnet he was of Barbadian origin and possibly felt sympathetic toward the prisoner. In any event the Governor dismissed him from office and offered a reward of £700 for Bonnet's recapture.

Bonnet managed to make contact with a small group of friends, who procured a boat and took him northward along the coast; but bad weather and shortage of food soon forced them to return to Sullivan's Island, near Charles Town. It was not long before word of their arrival there reached the ears of Governor Johnson, and he directed Colonel Rhett to take an armed party and seek out the fugitives. After a diligent search the Colonel's men found them, and opening fire, they killed Harriot and wounded two other members of the group. But Bonnet himself was taken alive and escorted the next day, November 6th, to Charles Town, where, this time, he was put into secure custody to await trial.

In the meantime, on Tuesday, October 28th, a Court of Vice-Admiralty had been convened for the trial of the pirates. Nicholas Trot, Judge of the Vice-Admiralty and Chief Justice of the Province of South Carolina presided, assisted by some ten other judges; and after the King's commission to Judge Trot had been read, a Grand Jury was sworn. The Judge then delivered a lengthy charge containing an extremely erudite account of the laws governing maritime trade and navigation and of their historical origins; and he enlarged particularly upon the crime of piracy which had come before the court for consideration.

The Grand Jury duly returned true bills against the accused, and a petit jury was then empanelled and sworn.

There were two indictments against Major Stede Bonnet and his 33 accomplices. One charged that on the second day of August in the fifth year of the reign of His Majesty, King George the First (1718) 'they did piratically and feloniously set upon, break, board and enter a certain merchant sloop, called the *Frances*, and did put her commander, Peter Manwaring, and his mariners in corporal fear of their lives, and piratically and feloniously did steal, take, and carry away the said merchant sloop, the *Frances*, with 26 hogsheads, 3 tierces, and 3 barrels of rum valued at 263 Pounds, 6 shillings, 3 pence, and other goods valued at Five Hundred Pounds.'

The second indictment accused them of having seized in a piratical and felonious manner the sloop *Fortune*, commanded by Captain Thomas Read, with her cargo of bread, linseed oil, hams, flour, and other goods.

Although all the prisoners, except three, pleaded 'not

guilty' they made practically no defence, but merely made excuses for their crimes, claiming they had been forced into committing these acts of piracy on account of finding themselves at sea in need of provisions. But the facts were plainly proved, and all the accused except four were found guilty.

Before pronouncing sentence of death, Judge Trot delivered a very solemn address to the prisoners concerning the seriousness of their crimes and their need for a sincere repentance. On Saturday, November 8th, the condemned men were all taken to the gallows at the White Point near Charles Town.

Two days later, when Bonnet himself was brought before the Court, he pleaded 'not guilty' to both charges of piracy, but he was convicted of one and next day he withdrew his plea to the other. In the course of the trial the Chief Justice pointed out how Bonnet, in company with Edward Teach, the infamous Blackbeard, had taken more than 28 vessels in the West Indies. He admonished him at great length concerning his numerous other acts of piracy, including 11 committed after he had received the King's pardon, and charged him also with being guilty of the murder of no fewer than 18 men who had been sent by lawful authority to apprehend him.

After this address, which was replete with quotations from Holy Scripture, Chief Justice Trot solemnly pronounced:

> 'That you, the said Stede Bonnet, shall go from whence you came, and from thence to the place of execution, where you shall be hanged by the neck till you are dead; And the God of Infinite Mercy be merciful to your soul.'

Under sentence of death the courageous attitude Bonnet had maintained all during his trial failed him, and he wrote a piteous letter to Governor Johnson pleading for his life. A number of his sympathisers similarly submitted a petition for clemency; but it was all in vain.

On Wednesday, December 10th, 1718, Major Stede

Bonnet, 'late of Barbados, Mariner', variously described as a gentleman, a man of fortune, man of letters, enemy of mankind, common robber and pirate, was carted in a semi-conscious state to the gallows at White Point, clutching a small posy of flowers in his manacled hands. His body was later buried beyond the low-water mark.

Apart from his genteel social background there is one factor that has made Stede Bonnet unique among pirates: he was the only one ever known to have bought his ship.

He has often been credited with having been the inventor of walking the plank – a method allegedly employed by pirates for toppling their victims into a watery grave. But the record of his trial contains no mention of this; and indeed, there is no evidence to support the legend that pirates used this form of punishment.

—— Captain Charles Vane ——

In July 1715 some ten Spanish galleons out of a fleet of eleven, on their way homeward from the Spanish Main loaded with silver, were wrecked by a great hurricane off the coast of Florida. Several vessels later sent from Cuba by the Spaniards succeeded in salvaging and taking away several million pieces of eight, but they were obliged to leave about 350,000 more in a storehouse under guard to await shipment.

Some time later five vessels, said to have been fitted out at Jamaica, Barbados, and elsewhere, landed 300 men at the site, overpowered the Spanish guard of 60 men, and carried off this rich hoard.

On returning from the raid the marauders moreover met and captured a Spanish ship on her way to Havana, and were highly delighted to find that in addition to a valuable cargo she had on board about 60,000 pieces of eight. But the Spaniards followed the raiders, and on seeing them enter a port in Jamaica they proceeded to Havana and notified the Governor, who immediately sent an envoy to the Governor of Jamaica complaining of the act of piracy and demanding the return of the stolen goods.

As Britain was then at peace with Spain the freebooters realised they could expect no protection from the Governor, but, on the contrary, were likely to be punished. So after disposing of their booty to good advantage, they equipped their vessels with plenty of ammunition and other necessary stores and took to the seas as pirates outright, plundering not only the ships of Spain, but also those of every other nation including their own.

Charles Vane

Before long they were joined by others, and they all decided that New Providence, one of the largest of the Bahama Islands, was the most suitable place at which to establish themselves, clean and repair their ships, and store their ill-gotten wealth.

As early as 1714 three groups of pirates had already established themselves in the Bahamas, and these islands, which then had no government, were soon swarming with these rogues, who included Edward Teach, alias 'Blackbeard', Benjamin Hornigold, Henry Jennings, and Thomas Burgess.

Prominent also in this community was Charles Vane. Very little appears to have been recorded concerning his origins and early life, but like Teach and many of the others he may have served in privateers during the recently concluded War of the Spanish Succession. He was, however, reputed to be one of those who had robbed the Spaniards of their silver in the Gulf of Florida.

Probably because he was overshadowed by more infamous figures such as Hornigold and Teach, Vane's earliest exploits as a pirate are also somewhat obscure and it appears that it was not until early 1718, when he was particularly active in the Gulf of Florida, that we find him beginning to receive special mention in the official reports on piracy in the Caribbean. This seems to have been mainly on account of his utter ruthlessness, for Vane was not content merely to plunder captured vessels; he quite frequently subjected their crews to the most brutal maltreatment.

This was particularly true in regard to vessels belonging to Bermuda, which made frequent voyages across to the Bahamas to take on salt. For example, Captain Edward North of the Bermudan sloop *William and Martha*, captured on April 14th, 1718, later reported how the crew of Vane's sloop, the *Ranger*, savagely beat him and his crew and tied one of them hand and foot down to the bowsprit, pushed a loaded pistol into his mouth and held burning matches to his eyes to force him to reveal what money there was on board.

Then the captain and crew of the sloop, *Samuel*, taken five days later near Crooked Island, one of the Bahamas, similarly reported having been given severe beatings after they had been robbed.

Another of Vane's victims was the sloop *Diamond*, taken off Rum Key (now Rum Cay), another of the islands. Her master, Captain Tibby and her crew were all robbed, and after brutally beating them, the pirates hanged one man up by his neck until they thought he was dead. Then seeing him beginning to revive, one of them struck him with a cutlass over the collar-bone, until another member of the gang intervened.

On July 26th, 1718 Captain Woodes Rogers, commissioned some months earlier as Governor and Vice-Admiral of the Bahamas, finally arrived at New Providence to take up his appointment, accompanied by His Majesty's ships, *Milford*, *Rose*, and *Shark*. Vested with complete authority to suppress piracy in the region, he brought with him the King's Proclamation offering pardon to all pirates who should surrender by the date specified in the Proclamation.

Rogers found that on the island there were nearly 1,000 pirates eagerly awaiting the long-expected pardon. But Captain Charles Vane, their leader, was contemptuous of any idea of surrender, and after converting a French prize he had taken into a fireship by loading a considerable quantity of gunpowder and inflammable materials on board, he cast her adrift after setting her on fire, and succeeded in driving the King's ship, *Rose*, out of the harbour. He then sailed out in his sloop with 90 hands on board, defiantly flying his black flag and firing his guns. The Governor sent two vessels in pursuit, but Vane succeeded in making good his escape.

Two days after his departure from New Providence Vane and his crew captured a sloop belonging to Barbados. He kept this vessel and put 25 hands on board, with one Yeats as captain. Then a day or two later they took another sloop, the *John and Elizabeth*, on her way into New Providence. She had on board a quantity of pieces of eight, and the pirates carried both these prizes to a small island, where they shared out the booty among themselves and spent some time living riotously in the manner of their kind.

After this, Vane sailed northwards in consort with Yeats and operated for a while on the shipping route between England and the North American Colonies. There they took several ships, and after pillaging them of their cargoes and valuables, allowed them to proceed.

The latter end of August found them off South Carolina, where they took and plundered several more vessels. One of these, a large brigantine inbound to Charles Town from Guinea, had more than 90 slaves on board, and Vane put these on board Yeats's vessel, much to the annoyance of his associate, before releasing the brigantine.

Yeats however had now become anxious to abandon his way of life, partly because Vane tended to treat him as an inferior, and one day shortly afterwards, while the two pirate vessels were at anchor off the coast, he suddenly slipped his cable, hoisted his sails, and speedily made off for the North Edisto River, a few miles south of Charles Town, where he and his crew surrendered themselves and received certificates of pardon. Infuriated at the desertion of his consort, Vane cruised for some time in the area in the hope of catching Yeats coming out again, but he was disappointed.

He did, however, manage to capture and plunder two vessels coming out of Charles Town. One of these later returned to port and reported the robberies, and two armed sloops that had been preparing to sail to the Cape Fear River in pursuit of some other pirates, set off on a diligent search southwards for Vane. Not finding him, they abandoned the search and proceeded to Cape Fear on their original mission.

Charles Vane had actually gone northwards to an inlet, where he happened to meet with Blackbeard, and after the two rogues had spent several days exchanging courtesies, Vane continued his voyage northwards to the seaboard of New York, where, in due course, he took a small number of prizes before sailing to the Windward Passage, between Cuba and Haiti.

On November 23rd, 1718, after he had been cruising

there for some time without sighting any vessel, he at last met a ship and immediately hoisted his black flag expecting her to surrender. But she responded instead by hoisting her own colours and delivering him a powerful broadside.

Vane had finally met his match, for she turned out to be a French man-of-war, and having had a taste of her superior fire-power, he decided to cut and run. His quartermaster, John Rackham, and the majority of his crew however felt confident that they could defeat and capture the Frenchman, but Vane did not agree, and since, as captain, his decision was final in such matters, his brigantine, which sailed faster than the man-of-war, soon left her far behind.

His flight from action led the majority of the crew to brand him a coward, and the next day they deposed him by vote and put him, together with those who had supported him, on board a sloop they had been holding as a prize and turned them loose with a supply of ammunition and provisions. They then voted John Rackham captain in Vane's place.

With his new vessel and smaller crew Vane now sailed for the Bay of Honduras, where they equipped themselves as best they could to continue their old trade, and later, off the north-west coast of Jamaica they took three small trading vessels. One of these (a sloop) they kept, and Vane put Robert Deal, the former mate of the brigantine, on board as her captain.

In mid-December, back in the Bay of Honduras, the pirates captured the *Pearl* of Jamaica and carried her off to Barnacko (now Bonacco), a small island, together with another sloop they took on the way. After spending some two months there, Vane set out on another cruise to the Bay, but a few days later a violent hurricane separated him from his consort and totally wrecked his sloop upon a small uninhabited island, and all his crew were drowned. Vane himself was saved, but unable to salvage anything from the wreck, he was quickly reduced to severe distress for want of necessities and managed to survive only through the charity of fishermen who frequented the island from the mainland to catch turtles.

While he was on this island a ship from Jamaica on her way down to the Bay called to take on a supply of water, and Vane, who happened to be acquainted with her captain, a former buccaneer by name of Holford, begged him to take him off. But Holford refused absolutely, telling him quite bluntly that if he took him on board, except as a prisoner, he would be sure soon to be conspiring with the crew to become pirates, and would knock him, Holford, on the head and run away with the ship.

Vane strongly protested having any such wicked intentions and repeated the most solemn reassurances; but Captain Holford, who knew his man far too well to place any faith in his words was adamant in his refusal and told him that if on his return to the island in about a month's time he found him still there he would carry him to Jamaica and see him hanged.

Vane then asked how he could get off the island, and Holford suggested that he might take one of the fishermen's dories. When Vane objected that this was stealing, Holford retorted that he was astonished that he, who was so notorious as a common robber and pirate, stealing ships of every kind and their cargoes and plundering all mankind, should suddenly become scrupulous about taking away so trivial a thing as a tiny row-boat. And with that Captain Holford departed and left Vane to fend for himself.

Soon afterwards, however, another ship called at the island to take on water for the voyage home, and as nobody on board knew who Vane was they took him on board as a shipwrecked sailor.

It seems that he had just begun to feel confident that he might escape being called to account for his crimes, when an accident put an abrupt end to his hopes. It happened that when Captain Holford was returning from the Bay of Honduras he met the vessel that had rescued Vane, and her captain, an old friend of Holford's, cordially invited him on board to dine. While on his way to the cabin Holford happened to glance down into the hold, and seeing Vane working there he immediately asked his host whether he knew whom he had on board. The captain replied that he had shipped a sailor from a trading sloop whom he had found shipwrecked on a certain island, and added that he seemed to be a 'brisk' hand.

He was amazed when Captain Holford informed him that the man was, in fact, none other than Charles Vane, the notorious pirate, and he readily agreed to deliver him into Holford's custody.

Captain Holford's mate later went and arrested Vane at pistol point and had him put in irons, and at Jamaica the prisoner was promptly delivered into the hands of the authorities.

Charles Vane was duly tried by a Court of Vice-Admiralty, convicted, and sentenced to death for his crimes, and on March 29th, 1719, he was taken to the place of execution at Gallows Point, Port Royal. According to an eyewitness, he 'betrayed [himself] the coward when at the gallows and died in agonies equal to his villainies', and 'he showed not the least remorse for the crimes of his past life.'

Captain Bartholomew Roberts

Bartholomew Roberts was born in 1682 in Pembrokeshire, Wales, and went to sea at an early age as an honest merchant seaman. In due course he became an expert navigator, and his exceptional skill eventually won him the position of Second Mate on the *Princess*, commanded by a certain Captain Plumb, which sailed from London for the Coast of Guinea, West Africa, in November 1719 to take on a cargo of slaves.

Shortly after the ship arrived in that area she was captured by Howel Davis, a pirate, and Roberts found himself a prisoner on board Davis's ship, the *Royal Rover*.

Like Roberts, Davis was of Welsh origin, and similarly had started life as a merchant seaman. But it seems he was villainously inclined, and on one occasion he was arrested and imprisoned at Barbados when his crew reported to the authorities that he had proposed that they become pirates. After holding him without trial for three months, the authorities had however found themselves obliged to release him since he had not actually committed any act of piracy.

After capturing the *Princess*, Davis continued his cruise along the Guinea Coast, trying all the while to persuade Roberts to join his crew, but Roberts completely disregarded the dazzling picture he painted of the fortune that awaited them in the Caribbean and elsewhere on the high seas.

However, it happened that before long Davis was killed while attempting to raid the Portuguese settlement at the Isle of Princes, and when the senior members of his crew, who styled themselves the Lords, voted to make Roberts their

Bartholomew Roberts with his ships the Royal Fortune *and the* Ranger

new leader, he cast all his scruples aside and took command of the *Royal Rover.*

His first act was to avenge Howel Davis by storming the Portuguese fort, jettisoning its guns into the sea, and bombarding the town. Then at night-fall he and his men put to sea by the light of two ships they had set on fire.

Sailing southward, they captured a Dutch ship and after plundering her they allowed her to go free. But an English vessel taken two days later was less lucky, for the pirates wantonly set her on fire and sank her after robbing her of whatever they wanted.

After taking on water and food supplies at the Island of Annabono they decided to set course for the coast of Brazil, where they arrived 28 days later. Roberts and his men cruised for several weeks without sighting a sail, and had just decided to sail north to the Caribbean when they unexpectedly came upon a Portuguese convoy of no fewer than 42 ships in the harbour of Bahia, all heavily laden and awaiting an armed escort to Lisbon. Sneaking in among this fleet, Roberts ordered the captain of the nearest vessel to come on board the *Royal Rover*, where by threats accompanied with much brandishing of cutlasses by his crew, he forced the Portuguese captain to point out the richest ship in the fleet. The pirates then boarded and captured this vessel after a brief fight.

This ship was found to be exceedingly rich. Besides a valuable cargo that included sugar and tobacco, she had on board 90,000 moidores besides jewellery of considerable value, including a cross of diamonds which had been intended for the King of Portugal. Successfully evading pursuit, Roberts and his men carried off their prize to Devil's Island, Cayenne, where they divided the spoil and spent some time making merry and trading with the inhabitants.

Bartholomew Roberts was, in some ways, a pirate of an unusual character that suggested some kind of religious upbringing. For one thing, he firmly believed in keeping the Sabbath; and in stark contrast to the majority of those of the pirate brotherhood, he detested strong drink, preferring tea, which he drank constantly in large quantities.

Shortly after taking command of the *Royal Rover* he drew up a set of Articles which had to be sworn to on the Bible and signed by every member of the crew. These prescribed, among other things, that all lights below deck were to be extinguished at eight o'clock at night. Anyone who wanted to drink after that hour had to do so up on the open deck. Gambling for money was forbidden, and no women were allowed on board. The penalty for smuggling a woman on board disguised as a man was death; and if any woman happened to be taken prisoner at sea, guards were to be posted to protect her from molestation.

The Articles also prohibited any fighting on board. All quarrels were to be settled on shore with sword or pistol under the supervision of the ship's quartermaster.

But whilst these and certain other measures were designed for the maintenance of discipline and order among the crew, some others were more or less related to their welfare, specifying how booty was to be shared out among officers and men, and fixing a scale of compensation for the various types and degrees of injury liable to be sustained in action. The ship's musicians were also made exempt from work on Sundays.

After leaving Devil's Island Roberts and his crew sailed for the West Indies, and arriving off the windward coast of Barbados in the middle of February 1720, they captured two vessels coming in from New York. One of these they decided to keep for themselves on account of her superior sailing qualities, and after fitting her out as a pirate ship with the guns and other equipment transferred from the *Royal Rover*, they gave the latter to her captain in exchange. The other vessel they plundered and held five of her crew prisoner; and after detaining the rest of the crew for three days they allowed them to proceed with their ship.

When these seamen arrived in port at Bridgetown on February 19th and reported the incident there was considerable alarm among the merchants, who were expecting several ships in from London and elsewhere. It happened that there was no naval ship on station at the time, so a group of these merchants immediately sought and obtained the Governor's permission to arm and equip two vessels at their own expense and send them in pursuit of the pirates.

These vessels sailed at dusk on the 22nd and finally caught up with the pirates four days later. In the running battle that followed Roberts came under such an intense bombardment he was finally forced to throw all his guns and heavy gear overboard to lighten his vessel and to put on all the sail she could carry in order to get away. He fled the scene vowing vengeance against Barbados and all its inhabitants, and it is said that whenever any ships belonging to that island fell in his way he was more ruthless to them than to any others.

Having lost about 35 of his men and suffered severe damage to his ship as well, Roberts made for the island of Dominica, where he replenished his supply of water and provisions and then departed for Carriacou, near the island of Grenada, to carry out major repairs. While he was there news of his presence reached the Governor of Martinique, who immediately sent two armed sloops after him; but when they arrived they found that he had left the island only a few hours earlier.

At this point, Roberts thought it might be prudent to depart for a safer area of operations - at any rate until the hue and cry had died down - so he set course for distant Newfoundland. He arrived there with his gang of cutthroats near the end of June, and they at once recommenced their deadly work by attacking all the shipping they found at the ports of Trepassy and St Mary's.

They entered the harbour at Trepassy with a blast of trumpets, with drums beating, and with their black flags fluttering boldly in the breeze. There were 22 ships at anchor, apart from smaller craft, and at the sight of the pirate ship their crews promptly abandoned them and fled ashore. The pirates then launched into an orgy of destruction, burning and sinking everything afloat, except one vessel they fancied for themselves, and then set about wantonly wrecking the installations the poor fishermen had erected for the drying and curing of their fish.

At St Mary's there were similar scenes of destruction, and altogether the toll of shipping destroyed at both ports amounted to 26 sloops and 150 fishing boats.

Although manned by about 1,200 men and equipped with 40 pieces of cannon, the shipping, through lack of leadership and courage, had failed to offer even the slightest resistance to the pirates, who numbered a mere 60 men in a single sloop armed with only 10 guns.

Bartholomew Roberts and his men, moreover, seized and occupied the port of Trepassy for two weeks, during which they compelled their prisoners to overhaul their vessel and to fit out the vessel they had captured for service as a pirate ship.

In this ship Roberts then took a cruise out upon the Grand Banks of Newfoundland, where he took some 10 French ships and destroyed all except one vessel of 26 guns. He kept this for himself, renamed her the *Royal Fortune*, and gave her captain his ship, which he had taken at Trepassy, in exchange.

A little later, with his sloop as consort to the newly acquired *Royal Fortune*, he took another cruise out on the Grand Banks, where he captured and looted several more ships, and then set out on a return voyage to the Caribbean, where he arrived in September.

By this time Roberts and his men had run short of supplies, and after cruising near the Island of Deseada (now Desirade) without capturing any vessel carrying provisions, they made for the island of St Christopher (now St Kitts). They boldly entered the harbour of Basseterre, the capital, and although they met with some opposition from shore batteries, they destroyed two ships, captured a third, and landed a party of men to round up and bring aboard some sheep.

Roberts then sent ashore an insolent letter informing the island's governor that had he done him the courtesy of coming on board the *Royal Fortune* and drinking a glass of wine with him and his crew, he, Roberts, would not have harmed the smallest vessel in the port.

The raid on St Christopher had, however, not proven very profitable to the pirates, so they went to the neighbouring island of St Bartholomew, where, for some reason, the authorities were pleased not only to provide them with everything they wanted, but also to entertain them with a great deal of hospitality.

Soon afterwards Bartholomew Roberts decided to return to the Guinea Coast, where he had begun his career as a pirate. En route he captured a French ship that was on her way to France from Martinique, and was delighted to discover that on board there was no less a personage than the governor of that island. Roberts gleefully had him hanged from the yardarm. He also found that apart from being loaded with a rich cargo, this ship was superior to his own vessel, the *Royal Fortune*, that he had taken off Newfoundland, so he took her for himself in exchange and renamed her also the *Royal Fortune*.

Roberts had intended touching at Brava, the southernmost of the Cape Verde Islands, to clean his new ship, but adverse winds forced him too far to the north, and finding it impossible to beat his way back southward he was forced to return to the Caribbean on the northeast trade wind.

On the return voyage the pirates suffered severely when they ran short of water, and were only saved from total disaster by a timely arrival on the coast of Surinam.

After replenishing their water supply Roberts and his men then made their way northwards to the West Indies, where they took two ships near Barbados. The mate of one of these, the *Greyhound*, joined the ranks of the pirates and eventually became captain of the *Ranger*, a vessel that later became consort to the *Royal Fortune*.

At the beginning of 1721, while engaged in wreaking considerable havoc among shipping in the Eastern Caribbean, Roberts got to hear about the two armed sloops the Governor of Martinique had sent down to Carriacou to destroy him, so he decided to strike a blow against that French island in reprisal. In mid-February, at St Lucia, he succeeded in capturing a heavily armed Dutch vessel after a hard fight. She was an 'interloper' - a vessel trading without licence in slaves, which she sold, like all of her kind, at bargain prices. This interloper suited Roberts's purpose admirably, and putting a number of his men on board, he sailed her under her Dutch colours close to the harbour at Martinique and hoisted the signals customarily employed by these vessels to attract customers.

In the course of the next two or three days some 14 sloops brought out planters and others who wanted to do business, only to find themselves taken by the pirates and relieved of the considerable sums of money they had on board. All the prisoners were then subjected to the most barbarous cruelties. Some were flogged almost to death, others had their ears cut off, and some others were tied to the yardarms and used as targets for pistol practice. Finally burning and sinking 13 of the vessels, the pirates packed their unfortunate victims on board the one that remained and sent them back ashore to tell the tale.

After this, Roberts and his crew of cut-throats roved at large among the islands, pillaging and destroying shipping of every description and nearly bringing all trade to a halt in the area. He could never overcome his anger at the attempts the authorities at Barbados and Martinique had made to destroy him, so he had a new flag made that ever afterwards he flew from the jackstaff of the *Royal Fortune*. This bore his own figure with a sword raised in his right hand and standing feet astride upon two human skulls. One of these had written beneath it the initials 'ABH', for 'A Barbadian's Head'; the other had 'AMH', for 'A Martinican's Head'.

After his operations in the West Indies, Roberts set sail once again for West Africa and took several prizes on the voyage down the coast. Near the River Senegal he defeated and captured two armed French ships that attacked him, mistaking him for an interloper intruding upon their monopoly of the slave trade in that area. He took them both to Sierra Leone, where he converted one into a storeship; and putting a crew on board the other, he renamed her the *Ranger* and made her consort to the *Royal Fortune*.

The pirates had arrived at Sierra Leone at the end of June 1721, and after spending several weeks there cleaning and refitting their ships they returned to sea at the beginning of August and resumed the pillaging of peaceable trading vessels, jettisoning any cargoes they didn't want, and occasionally burning and sinking captured vessels. After a while the *Onslow*, a fine ship belonging to the Royal Africa

Company, was taken, and Roberts, ever seeking to acquire a better ship than the one he happened to possess, kept her, equipped her with 40 guns, and changed her name to *Royal Fortune*. She was the third of his ships to bear that name, and he gave her captain his old French-built vessel of the same name.

When he captured the *Onslow* he found on board an Anglican clergyman who was on his way to take up an appointment as chaplain at Cape Corso Castle, and curiously enough, Robert's bloodthirsty gang wanted to retain him as their chaplain on board the *Royal Fortune*. Roberts offered him the position, assuring him that his only duty other than conducting religious services would be to make rum-punch for the crew. But the good parson declined the honour, and was allowed to go free after being relieved of three of his prayer-books and a corkscrew.

In the course of the following months the *Royal Fortune* and her consort, the *Ranger*, met with nothing but success. Finally, on January 11th, 1722 they entered Whydah (now Ouidah, Dahomey) - the *Royal Fortune* proudly displaying her notorious Jack bearing the initials ABH and AMH. In the harbour there were 11 ships at anchor - English, French and Portuguese - and all surrendered to the pirates without offering any resistance although at least three of them were each armed with 30 guns and manned by a crew of 100 men.

From each of the prizes Roberts demanded a ransom of eight pounds of gold dust; but one of them, the *Porcupine*, which had been engaged in taking on a cargo of slaves, refused to pay. Roberts, not the kind of man to tolerate such defiance, ordered his men to set her on fire, and 80 of the unfortunate slaves, chained together by twos, perished in the flames or were devoured by sharks if they succeeded in jumping overboard.

It was soon after this that Bartholomew Roberts received information that two ships of the Royal Navy, *HMS Swallow*, commanded by Captain Chaloner Ogle, and *HMS*

76

Weymouth, commanded by Captain Mungo Herdman, each of 60 guns, and recently arrived on the Guinea Coast as a protection against pirates, were searching for him. He hastily made for Annabono, but happening to miss that island, he decided to make for Cape Lopez, which he felt to be a place of safety.

On the morning of February 10th, the crew of the *Royal Fortune* were indulging in a bout of drunken revelry below deck, and Roberts was in his cabin enjoying a dish of salmagundi - a savoury concoction of pickled herrings, chicken, beef, and certain other ingredients - when one of his men rushed down from the deck and reported that he had seen a sail approaching. At first Roberts took no notice, thinking the approaching vessel to be either French or Portuguese; but when she was definitely identified as one of the King's ships he carefully dressed himself in the best outfit from his sea-chest. His waistcoat and breeches were of a rich crimson damask and there was a red feather in his hat. Around his neck a cross of diamonds hung suspended on a golden chain, a fine sword was in his hand, and across his shoulders was a silk sling containing a pair of pistols.

At his word of command the crew staggered up from below, cut the anchor cable, and hurriedly put on canvas. Roberts studied *HMS Swallow* carefully through his glass, and ever a highly skilled mariner, he rapidly decided to execute a manoeuvre that would have given him an excellent chance of making his escape. But the helmsman and most of his crew were too intoxicated to carry out his orders promptly, and the *Royal Fortune* soon found herself under heavy fire.

Presently Roberts was struck in the throat by a charge of grapeshot and killed instantly. Incredulous, the crew stared at his body; then they threw it over the side, clad in all its finery, in accordance with the wishes he had often expressed in his lifetime.

With their leader now dead, the pirates quickly lost courage. Many deserted their posts, and all foolishly neglected either to put up any defence or attempt to escape. One of the ship's flags, retrieved from beneath the fallen mast, portrayed the figure of a skeleton standing beside a man holding a flaming sword, indicating, as it were, a defiance of death itself. This flag was later introduced in evidence at the trial of the pirates, which began at Cape Corso Castle on March 28th and ended on the following April 2nd.

All the prisoners taken in the *Royal Fortune* and her consort, the *Ranger*, pleaded 'Not guilty' of piracy, but most were convicted. Some 52 were sentenced to death and later executed, while 20 were sentenced to penal servitude, 17 committed to prison in London, and 74 were acquitted.

In the action, 10 of the pirates had been killed in the *Ranger* and three in the *Royal Fortune*, while 19 later died of their wounds.

There is a certain irony in the fact that Captain Bartholomew Roberts, who hated and avoided strong drink all his life, met his death on account of it. However, in a career of piracy lasting a little above two years he had taken more than 400 ships - a record unequalled by any other pirate.

'In an honest service,' he reportedly once said, 'there is thin commons, low wages, and hard labour; in this, plenty and satiety, pleasure and ease, liberty and power; and who would not balance creditor on this side, when all the hazard that is run for it, at worst, is only a sour look or two at choking. No, a merry life and a short one shall be my motto.'

Bartholomew Roberts was only 40 years old when he was killed.

—Captain George Lowther—

Early in the year 1721 George Lowther sailed from London as second mate on board the *Gambia-Castle*, a large vessel of 250 tons, 16 guns and a crew of 30. She was owned by the Royal African Company, and in the month of May she arrived safely at her destination on the coast of Gambia, West Africa, where she disembarked a number of artisans and a detachment of soldiers under the command of a certain Captain Massey.

For some reason a bad relationship developed between Captain Charles Russell, the ship's master, and Lowther, and the latter managed to worm himself so well into the favour of the common sailors that one day when Captain Russell ordered him to be punished for some offence the men seized handspikes and threatened to knock down anyone who dared to lay hands on him. This, of course, served not only to widen the rift between the two officers; it also strengthened Lowther's attachment to the crew.

It was clear that these men were ripe for any kind of mischief and, abetted by Lowther, they grew insolent and insubordinate in their attitude to the captain and the chief mate even to the point of refusing to obey their orders.

One morning while the captain was ashore discussing this situation with the governor of the settlement and some of the merchants, Lowther had the chief mate confined and ordered the crew to prepare the ship for sailing; and later, when the captain had concluded his business Lowther refused to allow him back on board.

That same day the ship's company was joined by Captain

George Lowther

Massey and a number of the soldiers and artisans, who were all anxious to return to England because of conditions they had found intolerable - more particularly the meagre accommodation provided for them by the trading community, who controlled the place.

However, soon after the ship got to sea that afternoon Lowther assembled everyone on board and told them that it was the greatest folly to think of returning to England, for by seizing the vessel they had committed what in law was a capital crime. Therefore, he added, as they were a parcel of brave fellows and had a good ship under them it would be wiser for them to seek their fortunes upon the seas as other adventurers had done before them.

The company, numbering some 100 men besides the officers, quickly took the point and immediately set about such tasks as making structural alterations to the ship to fit her for her new role as a pirate vessel, and sewing up black flags.

Lowther renamed her the *Delivery* and drew up the following Articles which all hands were required to sign and, strangely enough, to swear to on the Bible:

'1.   The Captain is to have two full Shares; the Master is to have one Share and a half; the Doctor, Mate, Gunner and Boatswain, one Share and a quarter.

2.   He that shall be found guilty of taking up any unlawful Weapon on board the Privateer, or any Prize, by us taken, so as to strike or abuse one another, in any regard, shall suffer what Punishment the Captain and Majority of the Company shall think fit.

3.   He that shall be found Guilty of Cowardice, in the time of Engagement, shall suffer what Punishment the Captain and Majority shall think fit.

4.   If any Gold, Jewels, Silver, & c. be found on board of any Prize or Prizes, to the value of a Piece of Eight, and the Finder do not deliver it to the Quarter-Master, in the Space of 24 Hours, [he] shall suffer what Punishment the Captain and Majority shall think fit.

5.   He that is found Guilty of Gaming, or Defrauding another to the Value of a Shilling, shall suffer what Punishment the Captain and Majority of the Company shall think fit.

6.   He that shall have the Misfortune to lose a Limb, in time of Engagement, shall have the Sum of one hundred and fifty Pounds Sterling, and remain with the Company as long as he shall think fit.

7.   Good Quarters to be given when call'd for.

8.   He that sees a Sail first, shall have the best Pistol, or Small-Arm on board her.'

Apparently it was on July 20th, while about 70 miles off Barbados, that Lowther made his first capture. She was a brigantine belonging to Boston, Massachusetts, and after plundering her he sent her on her way.

Then two days later, 21 miles off the same island, he met another brigantine on her way into port. However, he made no attempt to take this vessel, but instead entrusted her captain with a letter and a document for delivery to the Governor of Barbados. This document, signed by himself and Massey, was a petition addressed to the King, explaining the circumstances that had caused them to run away from Gambia with the ship and asking for His Majesty's pardon.

But as they failed to surrender themselves to await the King's pleasure, the pirates clearly demonstrated that they had no serious intention of abandoning the lawless path they had chosen, and some days later, off Western Hispaniola, they captured a French sloop and relieved her of a considerable part of her cargo of wine, brandy, and other valuable merchandise.

Discord, however, soon reared its head among the company. It happened that Captain Massey, a professional soldier most of his life, wanted to take a party of men ashore to raid and pillage the French settlements, and became quite annoyed when Lowther pointed out the dangers involved and refused to agree to so rash an undertaking. The majority on board supported Lowther while the others sided with Massey, and one day a violent clash between these two factions was narrowly averted only by the timely appearance of a sail on the horizon.

The pirates immediately gave chase and finally caught up with the vessel, which turned out to be a small ship outbound from Jamaica to England. After they had plundered her of whatever goods they fancied and abducted two members of her crew, Lowther was for sinking her with everyone else on board, but Massey intervened and the vessel was allowed to go free.

The next day the pirates took a small trading sloop, which they kept with her cargo, and as Massey was still causing trouble and never tired of declaring his intention of leaving the company, Lowther gave him this vessel and he set course directly for Jamaica accompanied by the other malcontents.

There, he managed to convince the Governor, Sir Nicholas Lawes, that he had been an unwilling participant in Lowther's piracies and was glad when the opportunity finally came that enabled him to get away. When Massey furthermore volunteered to join a sloop fitted out to go in search of Lowther, he rose even higher in the Governor's esteem, and in due course Sir Nicholas Lawes provided him with a sum of money and a passage home.

Back in England in 1723, Captain Massey rather unwisely supplied a written account of all his piratical activities, not only to the Royal African Company but also to the Chambers of the Lord Chief Justice, and on July 5th he was brought to trial for piracy. Far from making any defence, he greatly strengthened the case against himself by confessing to at least two acts of piracy with which he had not been charged, and he was sentenced to death and hanged three weeks later.

Shortly after Captain Lowther had rid himself of his disagreeable partner, Captain Massey, he proceeded to the waters of the Eastern Caribbean, and near the island of Puerto Rico he encountered two ships which turned out to be a Spanish pirate and an English prize she had recently taken. At first Lowther threatened the Spaniards with death for having taken an English ship, but finally, after sending them away in their boat and enlisting the English sailors as pirates, he looted and then burnt both vessels.

A few days later his gang captured a small sloop belonging to the island of St Christopher (St Kitts), which they took with them to a small island. There, after careening and cleaning their own vessel, the *Delivery*, they remained for some time occupying themselves in 'unheard of debaucheries, with drinking, swearing, and rioting ... resembling devils rather than men; striving to outdo one another in new invented oaths and execrations.'

Putting to sea around Christmas of that year, 1721, the

pirates set course for the Bay of Honduras, and when they called at Grand Cayman Island to take on a supply of water they found a small vessel at anchor. She was manned by only 12 hands under the command of one Edward Low, and when Lowther and his crew discovered that this band were engaged in the same trade as themselves they treated them with considerable respect and invited them, on account of their small number, to join their ship, which they now called the *Happy Delivery*. Low readily accepted the invitation and was made second-in-command.

On January 10th, 1722, the pirates finally arrived in the Bay of Honduras and soon sighted the *Greyhound*, a ship of some 200 tons belonging to Boston and commanded by Captain Benjamin Edwards. Lowther immediately hoisted his black flag and fired a shot as a signal for her to surrender; but the only response he got was a broadside. After a fight that lasted an hour Captain Edwards found the pirate vessel too powerful an opponent, and knowing well that pirates were seldom disposed to show mercy to anyone who resisted them too long and too stubbornly he decided that it would be wise to haul down his colours.

And, most surely, after plundering the *Greyhound*, the pirates mercilessly set about whipping, beating, and cutting the members of her crew. Then they put them on board the *Happy Delivery* and set the *Greyhound* on fire.

During the rest of their cruise about the Bay of Honduras Lowther and his men captured six more vessels, which surrendered without offering any resistance. Three of these they destroyed, one they returned to her captain, and the other two they kept for themselves. One of these last, a sloop of 100 tons belonging to Rhode Island, Lowther fitted out with 18 guns and placed under Low's command.

His fleet, now numbering four vessels, including a tender, then sailed to the Bay of Amatique at the western end of the Gulf, where they carried ashore their sails to make tents and landed all their stores and their plunder. They then set to work careening and cleaning the ships. However one day they were suddenly attacked by a large body of the local Indians, and as they were in no condition to defend themselves they were forced to flee to two sloops that were afloat and abandon everything to their attackers, who soon set fire to their chief ship, the *Happy Delivery*.

Lowther and his company managed to equip the larger of the two vessels, the *Ranger*, as best they could, and everyone then went on board her and sailed for the West Indies, where they arrived at the beginning of May 1722.

The capture of a brigantine near the island of Deseada (now Desirade) with a cargo of badly needed provisions did much to revive their drooping spirits after their recent setbacks, and after sinking this vessel they went in to the island and replenished their supply of water for a voyage to North America.

Arriving off Virginia, the pirates captured the *Rebecca*, a brigantine belonging to Boston on her way in from St Christopher, and Lowther made Low her captain. At this point the two men decided to divide the company equally between themselves and go their separate ways, and Low departed with the brigantine and about 44 men.

Lowther continued his cruise northwards, and off New York he took three or four fishing boats. But these were of little value, and he and his crew were much happier when a ship they captured en route to New England from Barbados yielded them several hogsheads of rum and sugar, besides money, plate, and other valuable goods.

A ship they met later off the coast of South Carolina, however, brought them to the brink of disaster, for her captain refused to be intimidated when Lowther hoisted his dreaded black flag and fired the usual warning shot. On the contrary, he put up so fierce a resistance that Lowther soon found himself on the defensive and, in fact, finally had to run his vessel ashore to prevent her from being boarded. Unfortunately, when this brave captain went off in a boat with the intention of setting his grounded attacker on fire, he was shot from the shore by one of the pirates, and the mate was forced to stop pursuing them to return and take command of his ship.

Lowther eventually managed to get his sloop refloated; but she had been badly damaged and had suffered many casualties in the encounter, and he was obliged to take her to a secluded inlet in North Carolina, where he and the remnant of his crew remained several months inactive and lived off the surrounding country.

They were finally able to get away in the spring of 1723, and sailed for Newfoundland where they captured several vessels in a cruise on the Grand Banks.

Returning to the Caribbean in August, Lowther and his crew then cruised among the islands taking only a prize or two, which enabled them to replenish their dwindling stock of provisions.

Then in the evening of Saturday, September 14th, off Barbados, they met the *Princess*, a ship out of Guinea commanded by Captain Wickstead, and opened fire on her. After boarding the vessel they ransacked her and put lighted matches between the hands of the second mate and the surgeon to force them to disclose where the gold was concealed.

The pirates took 54 ounces of gold dust, all the ship's gunpowder and small arms, the remaining cargo, the gunner's and the boatswain's stores, as well as four pieces of cannon. Moreover, they forced two members of the ship's crew to join them, and five others signed their Articles voluntarily.

The *Princess* proved to be Lowther's last prize, apparently, for soon after she was taken he decided to seek a suitable place at which to careen and clean his sloop and plan fresh operations. The place chosen was the uninhabited island of Blanquilla, about 90 miles off the north coast of Venezuela and arriving there at the beginning of October, Lowther had the vessel's rigging removed and sent ashore, as well as all her guns and other moveable gear.

On October 5th the sloop *Eagle* of St Christopher,

commanded by Captain Walter Moor, happened to pass close to the island while on her way to Cumana, Venezuela, and Lowther's sloop was seen lying at anchor. Her careening had been completed, but her guns had not yet been replaced and she was not yet ready to return to sea. As Captain Moor knew that trading vessels did not usually call at this island he rightly concluded that this sloop could be nothing other than a pirate, and accordingly, he launched an attack.

After putting up a brief resistance the pirates, quite unprepared for action, surrendered, but Lowther and 12 members of the gang managed to escape out of the cabin window. Captain Moor and his men spent five days ashore hunting for them, but succeeded in capturing only five.

When he arrived at Cumana and made a report on these events the Spanish Governor sent a sloop out to Blanquilla with an armed party to seek out and bring in the remaining fugitives, and four of them were eventually caught, put on trial, and sentenced to slavery for life. Lowther and the last three still managed to evade capture, but some time later when some men from another sloop went ashore at the island they found him lying dead with a pistol beside him. The notorious terrorist of the high seas had committed suicide.

Captain Moor carried the captured pirate sloop to St Christopher together with several former members of her crew, and on March 11th, 1724 some 16 of them appeared before a Court of Vice-Admiralty charged with piracy. Three were acquitted and 13 were found guilty; but two of the latter were recommended to mercy by the Court and reprieved. On the following March 20th the remainder were taken to the gallows at the town of Old Road and hanged by the neck until dead.

The Governor of St Christopher, John Hart, reported to the Council of Trade and Plantations in London that they 'behaved themselves with greater marks of sorrow and contrition than is usually found amongst those wretched sett of people.'

Captain John Evans and His Crew

As a pirate leader, Captain John Evans was not of the first rank; nonetheless he enjoyed a certain amount of success in his relatively brief career, which began, rather unusually, not on the high seas but on land.

Like many of his more infamous contemporaries, notably Bartholomew Roberts and Edward Lowther, Evans began life as a peaceable mariner, and was for some time master of a trading sloop belonging to the island of Nevis. Later, on losing his employment, he went to Jamaica, where he obtained a position as mate of a vessel trading out of that island.

But the period was a lean one for seafaring men. The peace that, in 1713, had ended the long War of the Spanish Succession had thrown large numbers of them on to the job market; consequently, such individuals as John Evans as had been fortunate enough to obtain berths were paid rather low wages.

Apparently it was this that made him decide to embark upon piratical enterprises, as so many others had done, in an effort to make his fortune. In September 1722 he and three or four others of like mind got together, took possession of a canoe, and rowed from Port Royal to the north coast of Jamaica. There they landed, broke and entered one or two houses, and carried off money and moveable property in their canoe.

They had not found this adventure unprofitable, but of course their real ambition was to get out on the high seas where a real fortune was to be made. Obviously, a canoe was far from adequate, so they made their way along the coast keeping a careful look-out for a suitable vessel. It was at Dunn's Hole that they finally saw a sloop belonging to Bermuda lying at anchor. She was just the kind of vessel they were seeking, and the gang went boldly on board. Her crew were greatly astonished when Evans coolly announced that he was now their captain; but after a little discussion they agreed to join him, and the whole company then went off to a village nearby and spent the rest of the day celebrating in a tavern.

The innkeeper and his household were delighted to have such jovial customers, and assured them, when they were leaving, that they would be made welcome any time they cared to return. That same night they all returned, broke into the premises, and carried off everything they fancied.

Next day the gang mounted four guns in the sloop, renamed her the *Scowerer*, and set sail for Hispaniola. It was off the northern coast of that island that Evans took a Spanish sloop as his first prize. She proved to be rich, and the company being small, each man's share of the booty came to the substantial sum of £150.

They afterwards steered for the Windward Islands, and off Puerto Rico they took the *Dove*, a New England ship of 120 tons commanded by Captain Diamond, on her way to Jamaica. The pirates plundered the vessel, and after taking off the mate and two or three other hands to augment their numbers they allowed her to proceed. They then went in to one of the islands to take on water and other supplies and remained there for some time.

The next prize to fall to Evans and his crew was the *Lucretia and Catherine*, a vessel of 200 tons commanded by Captain Mills, which was taken on January 11th, 1723, near the island of Deseada (now Desirade), south of Guadeloupe. They kept her and sailed for Aves, a small island about 100 miles off the northern coast of Venezuela, where they intended to careen their own vessel. On approaching this island they sighted a sail and immediately went off in pursuit, but when they finally got within gunshot the pirates decided to abandon the chase for fear of losing contact with their prize, the *Lucretia*. They now found that they had got too far to leeward of Aves, so they made instead for the island of Aruba, where they dropped anchor.

The next day another prize fell easily into their hands when a Dutch sloop sailed in, unsuspecting of any danger, and was captured. Each man's share of the plunder was £50.

Evans found this vessel preferable to the *Lucretia*, which he then abandoned after taking off her mate, and thinking it risky to linger any longer in the area he set course with his company for Jamaica, where they captured a coastal vessel laden with sugar, before sailing for Grand Cayman, some 200 miles WNW.

So far, things had not gone too badly for them, but their adventures, unknown to them, were drawing to a close.

The company's boatswain was a disagreeable and quarrelsome fellow and as the Captain had frequently been obliged to reprimand him he developed a sense of grievance, considering himself ill-treated; not only did he abuse Evans, he also challenged him to meet him in a duel on the next shore they came to, as was the custom among pirates. But when the vessel finally reached Grand Cayman and Evans called upon him announcing that he was ready to take up the challenge, the boatswain refused not only to fight but even to go ashore, though it was he who had issued the challenge.

Captain Evans became enraged at what he saw as the man's cowardice, and seizing his cane he gave him a sound beating. This indignity was, however, much greater than the boatswain could bear, and drawing his pistol he shot the captain through the head, jumped overboard, and began swimming for the shore. But some of the men quickly manned a boat and went after him and brought him back on board.

The brutal killing of Captain Evans so infuriated the crew that they decided to torture the murderer to death, but while they were considering how best to deal with him, the ship's gunner drew his pistol and shot him through the body. The shot, however, did not prove fatal and the boatswain pleaded to be granted a week's respite to repent of his crime. But no one thought him deserving of any consideration, and with an oath another member of the crew approached him and shot him dead without any further ado.

With the captain dead there was only one other man on board who understood navigation, and that was the mate of the *Lucretia* whom they had taken and were holding prisoner. The pirates invited him to take command of the vessel, but he declined, and they now had no other choice than to break up the company. The gang, numbering some thirty hands, then went ashore at Grand Cayman taking about £9,000, which they shared out among themselves. The *Lucretia's* mate then took charge of the vessel, and with the assistance of the ship's boy, he managed to sail her safely to Port Royal, Jamaica.

— Captain Francis Spriggs —

Francis Spriggs is reputed to have sailed from London in the *Gambia Castle* in March 1721 in company with George Lowther, and was one of the men who joined him when he seized control of the vessel on the West African coast the following June and set off on his piratical adventures.

Spriggs became quartermaster to Lowther and Edward Low, who later joined the ship as Lowther's chief lieutenant, and participated fully in all the robberies and barbarities committed by this infamous pair. Then in late May 1722 when Low took command of the captured brigantine *Rebecca* and separated from Lowther, Spriggs elected to join his company; and he sailed with Low until near the end of the following year.

It appears that, around Christmas, the two men had a bitter disagreement about whether a member of the crew who had murdered another in cold blood should be hanged, and when they captured the *Delight*, a ship of 12 guns, off the coast of Sierra Leone, West Africa, Spriggs took possession of her and sailed off for the Caribbean together with about 60 hands.

Next day the crew elected him captain, and he had a copy of Edward Low's black flag, called the 'Jolly Roger', made and he hoisted it at the ship's mast-head. This bore the device of a white skeleton holding in one hand an hour-glass and in the other an arrow piercing a bleeding heart.

On their way to the West Indies, Spriggs and his gang met a Portuguese vessel, and after relieving her of her cargo, they decided to amuse themselves a little by subjecting her crew to an ordeal called 'sweating'. Lighted candles were placed in a circle around the mizzen-mast between decks, and each Portuguese in turn was made to run around and around the mast for about ten minutes while the pirates formed a circle outside and jabbed him with swords, knives, forks, compasses, and other pointed implements. Naturally these cut-throats considered this procedure great fun, and when the 'sweating' was finally over they cast the Portuguese adrift in a boat with a small quantity of provisions and set their vessel ablaze.

Later, while cruising off the island of St Lucia, Spriggs and his men captured a sloop belonging to Barbados which they plundered and then burned. They forced some of her crew to sign their Articles, and others who refused were brutally beaten and lacerated and finally turned adrift in a boat. They eventually managed to return safely to Barbados.

Shortly after this, Captain de Haws had his ship taken and plundered within sight of Barbados, and the pirates forced two of his crew to join them before they released his vessel.

The next capture was a vessel belonging to Martinique. Her crew were maltreated in the usual manner, but were allowed to keep their ship and continue on their way.

Spriggs afterwards sailed to the Bay of Honduras and made two or three more captures before taking his vessel to a small island for careening. Then he steered a course for St Christopher, back in the West Indies, intending to lie in wait for Captain Moore, Commander of the sloop *Eagle* belonging to that island.

The previous October, Moore had surprised George Lowther while he was careening and cleaning his vessel at the island of Blanquilla and had put an end to his career of robbery on the high seas, and now Spriggs was anxious to get the gallant captain in his clutches and avenge his former associate in crime.

But instead of the *Eagle* he ran into a French man-of-war cruising off the coast, and preferring to avoid such company, he promptly put on all sail and made off northwards at high speed with the Frenchman in hot pursuit. Fortunately for Spriggs, the man-of-war lost her main-topmast during the chase and he succeeded in getting away.

We next hear of Spriggs operating off Bermuda where, on April 30th, 1724, he took and pillaged a New York schooner. He coolly boasted to Captain Richardson, her Master, that he intended to ravage the northern coasts and sink every vessel he captured north of Philadelphia.

Two days later the brigantine *Daniel* of Boston, commanded by Captain John Hopkins, was also taken, and she was set on fire after the pirates had plundered her and forced two members of her crew to sign their Articles. Spriggs swore to Captain Hopkins that he intended to 'increase his Company on the Banks of Newfoundland' and then sail for the coast of New England in search of Captain Peter Solgard of His Majesty's ship *Greyhound*, who the previous June had defeated and captured his fellow pirate, Charles Harris, Low's consort, and had delivered him and his crew to justice.

Spriggs, however, did not sail to Newfoundland after all. Instead he returned to the Caribbean and on June 4th, windward of St Christopher, he took a sloop belonging to the island of St Eustatia. After his men had plundered this vessel of such cargo as she was carrying they fancied a little entertainment; so they fastened ropes around the bodies of her crew and repeatedly hoisted the men as high as the main - and fore-tops and let go of the ropes causing them to crash on to the deck. Then after whipping the crippled men along the deck they returned the sloop to the Captain and told him to go.

About a week after this another ship was taken on her way into St Christopher from Rhode Island. Besides her normal cargo of provisions she had some horses on board, and the pirates mounted these and rode them backwards and forwards about the deck at full gallop, all the while cursing, swearing and yelling like demons. This soon made the animals so wild that they threw off their riders and spoiled their fun. At this the pirates turned upon the ship's crew and whipped, beat and cut them mercilessly, saying that it was because they had not brought boots and spurs with the horses they (the pirates) were unable to ride like gentlemen.

A man seldom lacking in boldness, Captain Spriggs next appeared off Port Royal, Jamaica, and seized at least one vessel in sight of land. Two of His Majesty's ships, the *Diamond* and the *Spence*, then in port, weighed anchor and sailed off in pursuit, but they failed to find him. The *Spence* returned to Port Royal, but Captain Wyndham of the *Diamond* decided to proceed to the Bay of Honduras, suspecting that this was where Spriggs would most likely be found.

He proved to be correct, for when the *Diamond* arrived in the Bay he found Spriggs and his crew there busily occupied in plundering some 10 or 12 vessels that had come to load log-wood. Spriggs had as consort a sloop he had lately captured and put in command of one Shipton with about 40 hands, and the entire company were taken completely by surprise when the King's ship appeared unexpectedly and opened fire.

The pirates fired a few shots in a feeble reply, but quickly decided that it would be wiser to flee the scene as speedily as possible. There was little wind at the time, so they got out their oars and rowed into shallow water where they couldn't be followed, and in that way they were able to make their escape.

After this narrow brush with disaster, Spriggs and Shipton set off together for North America by way of the Bahama Channel and during the voyage they ran very short of provisions. On the way they captured a sloop sailing from Havana to Jamaica with a cargo of slaves, whom they took on board their two vessels. But this merely caused a further depletion in their meagre food supply, and later when Spriggs took another vessel that was bound for New England he proposed to put all the slaves on board her. Her captain however explained that he too was short of food and they would perish by starvation if he took them all. Spriggs then

A Spanish ship sinks a pirate craft

gave him only ten of the slaves and let him go, and he made his way to South Carolina to obtain provisions.

Afterwards, off Rhode Island, Spriggs met another vessel, which he plundered in the usual manner. Then after taking off the mate and all the rest of her crew he put the remaining slaves on board and left her master, Captain Durffie, to manage them as best he could.

Spriggs and Shipton had been able to re-provision their ships out of the vessels they had recently plundered, but cold weather and heavy gales soon forced them to return to the warmer waters of the Bay of Honduras.

Spriggs and his consort, Shipton, next left for the Bahamas, but when they reached the western end of Cuba they had the misfortune once again to encounter His Majesty's ship *Diamond*, which was still searching for them. As on the previous occasion, they decided to make a run for it, and the King's ship chased them over to the coast of Florida, where Shipton's sloop ran aground and was lost. All his crew got safely to shore, only to fall into the hands of the Indians, who reputedly killed and ate 16 of them and carried some 49 others off to Cuba. About £2,000 worth of gold fell prize to the *Diamond*.

Spriggs, by good seamanship, was able to escape, and in some way afterwards picked up Shipton and the few men who had escaped with him. Soon the two men were back in the Bay of Honduras, where on December 23rd, 1724, they took and plundered 16 vessels. They burned one of these after turning her captain and crew adrift in a boat.

In April 1725 Spriggs was reported to be in command of a small fleet of five ships, and was operating off the coast of Carolina, but his movements and activities after this are obscure.

A year later a rumour reached Boston, Massachusetts, that Spriggs and Shipton had both been marooned by their men and 'were got among the Mosquito Indians', on the coast of Honduras. And that was the last heard of them.

—— Captain Edward Low ——

Edward Low was a pirate whose record of brutality places him firmly in the class of the demonic buccaneer, Francis L'Ollonois. Born in Westminster, London, and totally illiterate, he started quite early on his criminal career by extorting small coins from the other boys of his neighbourhood.

Certain members of his family were also criminally inclined, and one of his brothers, who began with petty thievery at the tender age of seven and graduated in due course to housebreaking and burglary, ended his life on the gallows before reaching maturity.

When Edward himself reached manhood he migrated to Boston, Massachusetts, where he worked for a while as a ship-rigger before embarking in 1721 as a sailor on board a sloop bound to the Bay of Honduras to cut and take on a cargo of logwood. On the vessel's arrival he was placed in charge of a boat with a working party of 12 men, and one day when they returned to the ship before dinner was ready and the captain asked them to make another trip ashore in order to save time they all became angry, and in a fury Low seized a musket and fired at him. The shot missed the captain, but struck another man through the head, and at this Low and his companions took to the boat and put to sea.

The party now decided to become pirates, and the next day they captured a small vessel, made themselves a black flag, and sailed to the island of Grand Cayman, about 200 miles WNW of Jamaica, to equip themselves for their new calling.

Edward Low

An account has already been given of the manner in which the newly-fledged pirate George Lowther met them there and persuaded them to join his company, making Low his second-in-command. And we have seen how the two men operated together until on May 28th, 1722, when off Virginia, Low, together with a part of the crew, left the company when he was given a captured brigantine.

It was six days later that he took two prizes, which he plundered of their provisions. One of them, a sloop taken off Rhode Island on her way into port, he disabled by cutting away her sails and rigging to prevent her from reaching her destination and reporting the piracy; but nonethless she managed to alert the authorities by sending in a whale boat. Two armed vessels were sent in search of Low, but they returned some days later without having sighted him.

Low had taken the precaution of getting away from the coast, but around July 12th he sailed boldly into the harbour at Marblehead, Massachusetts, where he found 13 ships at anchor. Hoisting his black flag, he ran in among them threatening to give no quarter to any who offered resistance. Low plundered every one of them and then released all except a schooner of 80 tons that he fancied. After equipping her with 10 guns and a crew he named her the *Fancy*, took command as captain, and placed one Charles Harris in command of the brigantine.

With their numbers heavily augmented by a number of new hands enlisted by force or persuasion from among the ships at Marblehead, the pirates now set course for the Caribbean and finally arrived safely at a small island in the Leewards after surviving a severe battering by a hurricane.

After the two vessels had been refitted and provisioned as well as circumstances permitted, the brigantine sailed out on a short cruise and, a few days later, met a ship that had recently sailed from Barbados. She had lost her masts in the recent hurricane and was making her way slowly to Antigua for refitting, so the pirates naturally found her easy prey and robbed her of about £1,000 in money and goods.

When the brigantine returned and rejoined the schooner the two pirate leaders decided that it would be prudent to leave the area to avoid any possible encounter with any of the naval vessels stationed in the West Indies, and accordingly they proceeded eastward to the Azores, where several ships surrendered peacefully when Low threatened to give no quarter to any who offered resistance.

One crew that did attempt to defend their ship were savagely cut and maimed when their vessel was taken, and two Portuguese friars found on board were triced up and repeatedly hoisted high in the air and let down violently until they expired. Another passenger, who showed sorrow at these barbarous proceedings, aroused the anger of one of the pirates, who turned on him remarking that he did not like his looks, and delivered him a blow across the stomach with his cutlass that disembowelled him. The man fell dead without uttering a sound.

After taking a cruise among the Canary Islands without taking any prey, the two pirate ships made for the Cape Verde Islands, where they captured and plundered several vessels. But here the brigantine capsized while being careened and her crew were obliged to embark on the schooner, the *Fancy*, for the return voyage to the Caribbean.

They hadn't travelled very far when they sighted a Portuguese ship homeward-bound from Brazil and gave chase. They finally captured her after a fight, and by torturing several of the crew to make them reveal where money and valuables were hidden Low learned that during the chase the captain had hung a bag containing 11,000 gold moidores, approximately equivalent to £15,000, out of the cabin window and had let it drop into the sea immediately the ship was captured. Low flew into a rage at having been cheated of this rich bounty, and he ordered the captain's lips to be sliced off forthwith and broiled before his face. Then he had him and all the 31 members of his crew massacred in cold blood.

Finally arriving in the northern part of the Caribbean, Low cruised for about one month, taking at least four vessels. He burnt one of these for no other reason than that she belonged to New Englanders, whom he hated; then, after careening and cleaning his schooner in one of the islands, he set sail for the Bay of Honduras.

Just as he arrived on March 10th, 1723, he met a sloop

101

making her way out. Immediately he hoisted Spanish colours, but as soon as he got close he hauled them down, ran up his black flag, and fired a broadside. Then he closed in alongside and his men leapt on board.

This vessel, a Spanish privateer of six guns and about 70 men, had that morning captured and pillaged several New England vessels and taken their captains prisoner; and when the pirates went into the hold and discovered these prisoners, as well as a quantity of English goods, Low furiously ordered them to kill all the Spaniards.

Immediately they fell upon their defenceless captives with cutlasses, axes, swords, and pistols. Those who ran down into the hold seeking refuge were pursued and slaughtered, and those who jumped overboard and began swimming for the shore were pursued in a canoe and knocked on the head. Only 12 managed to reach the shore. Altogether some 45 of the Spaniards were killed, and the pirates then set their vessel on fire and sank her.

Later, while they were on shore drinking and enjoying themselves, one badly wounded Spaniard crawled weak and faint out of his hiding place and pleaded piteously for mercy. In response, one of the cut-throats forced the man to his knees, thrust the muzzle of a loaded musket into his mouth, and squeezed the trigger.

Low duly restored the New England captains to their ships, but concerned lest news of his whereabouts should reach any vessel of the King's navy, he would not allow them to proceed to Jamaica, their destination, but, by threatening to kill any of them he should happen to meet again if his orders were disobeyed, he forced them to steer instead for New York.

After this Low cruised off the Leeward Islands and took six vessels before setting course for North America. Off South Carolina, around the end of May, in consort with Harris, who was now in command of another sloop, the *Ranger*, he captured several prizes. On discovering that one of these, the *Amsterdam Merchant*, belonged to New England he not only looted her of her cargo; he also gleefully cut off the ears of her captain, slit his nose, and cut him about the body. Then he sank the ship.

In another instance, because he had taken a dislike to the captain of another prize, Low had burning matches - the kind used for touching off the guns - tied between the fingers of his crew, burning the flesh off the bones. Then, after having the men slashed about their bodies with cutlasses and knives and robbed of all their provisions, he put some of them ashore on an uninhabited part of the coast.

So far, Low's piratical exploits had proved very profitable,

Low presenting a pistol and bowl of punch (The Pirates' Own Book *1842)*

for at this time he was reputed to have on board no less than £80,000 in gold and silver. It happened that one of his victims had reported his activities to His Majesty's ship *Greyhound*, based on the New York station, and she put to sea to search for him and his associate, Charles Harris. The King's ship and the two pirate vessels finally sighted each other on June 10th, 1723, and the two pirate captains, ever on the lookout for prey, promptly gave chase.

For several hours the *Greyhound* lured them on; then when they finally came within gunshot she went into action with her powerful armament of 30 guns. Soon Harris's sloop was disabled, and with 12 of his men killed, he hauled down his black ensign and surrendered. At this, Low who hitherto had enjoyed a reputation for courage and boldness, now showed the stuff he was really made of by cravenly making off as fast as his ship could sail, abandoning his friend to his fate. The *Greyhound* carried the *Ranger* into Rhode Island and delivered Harris and the remnant of his crew into the hands of the jubilant authorities.

At a Court of Vice-Admiralty held at Newport from the following July 10th to July 12th, 25 of the prisoners out of the 35 taken, including Harris, were found guilty of piracy and sentenced to death and were finally executed on July 19th. Two others were also found guilty but were recommended for mercy, while eight were acquitted.

Captain Peter Solgard, the commander of *HMS Greyhound*, was greatly honoured by the city of New York for his achievement in capturing these freebooters and bringing them to justice.

As Edward Low fled from the fight with the King's ship he heaped a multitude of curses upon her and swore to take vengeance upon everyone he should capture from then on. This was no idle threat, and when he took a whaling sloop two days later some 80 miles off the coast he had her captain stripped naked and whipped about the deck, had his ears cut off, and finally had him shot through the head. The crew were put into a whale boat with a compass and some biscuits and water and their vessel was sunk.

Then when he took a fishing boat two days after this, Low cut off the head of her captain. But this was merciful in comparison with the fate suffered by his next victims - the captains of two whaling sloops taken off Rhode Island. One of them was ripped open alive and disembowelled; his heart was then roasted and the mate was made to eat it. The other captain, after being savagely slashed about his body, had his ears cut off and roasted and he was forced to eat them with salt and pepper. The unfortunate man afterwards died of his injuries.

Low then set sail north to Newfoundland, but paused and cruised for a while off Cape Breton, where he seized and pillaged 23 French vessels. One of the larger of these he kept and provided with a crew selected out of his own ship, and the two vessels proceeded to Newfoundland, where they took 18 more vessels in the harbours and out on the Grand Banks and sank some of them.

Towards the end of July 1723 Low captured a large ship from Virginia called the *Merry Christmas*, and after equipping her with 34 guns by opening several additional ports in her hull, he went on board and took command, styling himself Admiral, and hoisted a new black flag bearing the device of a human skeleton in red.

He then decided to make a return cruise to the Azores, arriving there about September 1st, and the first vessel taken was a brigantine, formerly English, but recently purchased by a Portuguese nobleman. Low found that she was manned partly by English sailors and partly by Portuguese, and he had all the latter hanged and the English put into their ship's boat and cast adrift. Then he set the brigantine on fire and sank her.

At St Michael's (Sao Miguel), one of the islands, he sent his men in boats into the roadstead to cut out an English ship. As she carried 14 guns and was therefore considerably more powerful than all the pirate boats together, her captain tried to get his crew to put up a defence; but they refused either out of cowardice or because of an inclination themselves to join the ranks of the pirates, and the captain was obliged to surrender. When he was taken on board Low's ship his ears were sliced off close to his head because he had dared to call upon his men to offer resistance, and his ship was sunk.

The crew of another vessel taken not long after this fared somewhat better than usual, for the pirates merely inflicted a few cuts on them here and there and then set them adrift in their boat before burning their ship.

Low's flotilla next took a cruise among the Canaries and the Cape Verde Islands and then sailed for West Africa where, on October 27th, off Sierra Leone, they captured the *Delight*, an English ship out of London. She carried 12 guns, and having formerly been a man-of-war she suited Low admirably. He mounted four more guns in her, manned her with 60 men, including 16 of her own crew whom he forced to join his company, and put his quartermaster, Francis Spriggs, on board as captain. Two days later, however, Spriggs sailed off into the night, deserting his 'Admiral', and went off 'a-pirating' on his own account.

Edward Low's activities during the following three or four months are somewhat obscure, but it appears that much of this time was spent on a cruise along the coast of South America. What, however, is certain is that early in 1724 he was operating again in the Caribbean, because on March 25th that year Governor John Hart of the island of St Christopher wrote to the Council of Trade and Plantations in London stating:

'I do not hear that there are any more pirates, except a ship commanded by one Lowe with about fifty pirates in his crew . . .'.

After recounting some details of various atrocities reportedly committed by Low against the Spaniards and the Portuguese, the Governor concluded:

'This Lowe is notorious also for his cruelty even to the subjects of the British Nation; and as a greater monster never infested the seas, I submit it to your Lordships' superior judgement whether it ought not to be recommended to His Majesty that a Proclamation be issued, even with pardon to his accomplices, offering an ample reward to such as should bring him in alive or dead.'

On the following May 17th some sailors arrived at Barbados after suffering much hardship, and reported how they had recently been taken near St Lucia by Low, who at that time had only 30 men with him.

Apparently it was not long after this that he got into a quarrel with his crew, and when the quartermaster took sides against him he became so enraged that he murdered the man in his sleep. This led to his undoing, for the crew at once rose up against him and threw him, together with two or three of his supporters, into a boat without any provisions and turned him adrift.

A day later Low and his companions were picked up by a French vessel and taken into Martinique, where they were speedily tried, condemned, and hanged for their crimes against humanity in general and the French in particular.

Thus ended the career of Edward Low whose record of cruelty was unmatched by any other sea rover, including even the ferocious 'Blackbeard', during the so-called 'golden age of piracy'.

Appendix

Proclamation Under Which Blackbeard, Hornigold, Bonnet, and Hundreds of Other Pirates Surrendered

By the King
A Proclamation for Suppressing of Pyrates

Whereas we have received Information, that several Persons, Subjects of Great Britain, have, since the 24th Day of June, in the Year of our Lord, 1715, committed divers Pyracies and Robberies upon the High-Seas, in the West-Indies, or adjoining to our Plantations, which hath and may Occasion great Damage to the Merchants of Great Britain, and others trading into those Parts; and tho' we have appointed such a Force as we judge sufficient for suppressing the said Pyrates, yet the more effectually to put an End to the same, we have thought fit, by and with the Advice of our Privy Council, to Issue this our Royal Proclamation; and we do hereby promise, and declare, that in Case any of the said Pyrates, shall on, or before, the 5th of September, in the Year of our Lord 1718, surrender him or themselves, to one of our Principal Secretaries of State in Great Britain or Ireland, or to any Governor or Deputy Governor of any of our Plantations beyond the Seas; every such Pyrate and Pyrates so surrendering him, or themselves, as aforesaid, shall have our gracious Pardon, of, and for such, his or their Pyracy, or Pyracies, by him or them committed, before the fifth of January next ensuing. And we do hereby strictly charge and command all our Admirals, Captains, and other Officers at Sea, and all our Governors and Commanders of any Forts, Castles, or other Places in our Plantations, and all other our Officers Civil and Military, to seize and take such of the Pyrates, who shall refuse or neglect to surrender themselves accordingly. And we do hereby further declare, that in Case any Person or Persons, on, or after, the 6th Day of September, 1718, shall discover or seize, or cause or procure to be discovered or seized, any one or more of the said Pyrates, so refusing or neglecting to surrender themselves as aforesaid, so as they may be brought to Justice, and convicted of the said Offense, such Person or Persons, so making such Discovery or Seizure or causing or procuring such Discovery or Seizure to be made, shall have and receive as a Reward for the same, viz. for every Commander of any private Ship or Vessel, the sum of 100 Pounds for every Lieutenant, Master, Boatswain, Carpenter, and Gunner, the Sum of 30 Pounds and for every Private Man, the sum of 20 Pounds. And if any Person or Persons, belonging to, and being Part of the Crew, of any such Pyrate Ship and Vessel, shall, on or after the said sixth Day of September, 1718, seize and deliver, or cause to be seized and delivered, any Commander or Commanders, of such Pyrate Ship or Vessel, so as that he or they be brought to Justice, and convicted of the said Offence, such Person or Persons, as a Reward for the same, shall receive for every such Commander, the sum of 200 Pounds which said Sums, the Lord Treasurer, or the Commissioners of our Treasury for the Time being, are hereby required, and desired to pay accordingly.

Given at our Court, at Hampton-Court, the fifth Day of September, 1717, in the fourth Year of our Reign.

George R.

God save the King.

Glossary

Brigantine	A two-masted merchant ship, square-rigged on the fore-mast and fore-and-aft rigged on the main-mast. Could mount about 12 cannon and carry a crew of 100.
Careen	To heel a ship over on her side to clean or caulk her.
Freebooter	A pirate or buccaneer. An adventurer who makes a business of plundering.
Man-of-war	A three-masted, square-rigged vessel, usually exceeding 300 tons. Employed as a naval vessel and armed with about 60 guns, and carrying a crew of about 200.
Moidore	Former Portuguese gold coin.
Piece of eight	A Spanish silver piece of eight reales or royals, worth about five English shillings. First minted in Spain about 1498, and later also in Spanish America.
Schooner	A two or three-masted vessel fore-and-aft rigged on all the masts. Of shallow draught, it enabled pirates to navigate shoal waters and hide in remote coves.
Sloop	A one-masted vessel, fore-and-aft rigged with a long bowsprit. Much favoured by pirates because its shallow draught enabled it to manoeuvre in channels. Could carry 12 to 14 cannon and a crew of about 75.

Bibliography

Botting, Douglas and the Editors of Time-Life Books, *The Pirates* Time-Life Books, Alexandria, Virginia, 1978.

Calendar of State Papers, Colonial, America and the West Indies. (Preserved in the Public Record Office), Vols XXVII-XXXVII. Edited by Cecil Headlam, London, 1927-1937. Currently reprinted by Kraus Reprint Corporation, Millwood, New York, 10546. U.S.A.

Carse, Robert. *The Age of Piracy* Robert Hale Ltd, London, 1959.

Defoe, Daniel. *A General History of the Pirates* Edited by Manuel Schonhorn. Originally published in 1724. Reprinted by Messrs J.M. Dent & Sons Ltd, London 1972.

Dictionary of National Biography. Edited by Sir Leslie Stephen and Sir Sidney Lee. Oxford University Press, London, 1949-50.

Dow, George Francis and Edmonds, John Henry. *The Pirates of the New England Coast, 1630-1730* Originally published in 1923. Reprinted by Argosy-Antiquarian Ltd, New York, 1968.

Exquemelin, Alexander O. *The Buccaneers of America* Originally published in 1678 in Dutch. Translated by Alexis Brown. Republished by Penguin Books, London 1969.

Gosse, Philip. *The Pirates' Who's Who* Dulan & Co. Ltd, London, 1924.

Gosse, Philip. *The History of Piracy* Cassell & Co. Ltd, London, 1932. Second Printing 1954.

Hughson, Shirley C. *The Carolina Pirates and Colonial Commerce, 1670-1740* John Hopkins Press, Baltimore, 1894.

Johnson, Captain Charles. *A General History of the Robberies and Murders of the Most Notorious Pirates* First published in 1724. Edited by Arthur L. Hayward, 1926. Reprinted by Routledge & Kegan Paul, London, 1954.

Lee, Robert E. *Blackbeard The Pirate* John F. Blair, Winston-Salem, North Carolina, 1974. Second Printing 1976.

Masefield, John. *On the Spanish Main* Conway Maritime Press Ltd, London, 1906. New Edition, 1972.

112

Rawlin, William. *The Laws of Barbados* Collected in one volume. London, 1699.

State Trials, Vol. VI, A complete collection of State Trials and proceedings for high treason and other crimes and misdemeanours. Fourth Edition. Printed by I. Wright ... for C. Bathurst (and others) and sold by G. Kearsby ... 1776 (-1781)

Unpublished Letters and Documents

Colonial Office Class 28 (Barbados) Original Correspondence with the Council of Trade and the Secretary of State.

C O 28/17   folio 197
C O 28/18   folios 23 and 44

Minutes of the Barbados Council, 8 August 1721